WORLD BANK INDEPENDENT EVALUATION GROUP

IEG

Annual Review of Development Effectiveness 2006

Getting Results

2006
The World Bank
Washington, D.C.

http://www.worldbank.org/ieg

ISSN: 1520-9733
ISBN-10: 0-8213-6906-7
ISBN-13: 978-0-8213-6906-7
e-ISBN:0-8213-6907-5
DOI: 10.1596/978-0-8213-6906-7

World Bank InfoShop
E-mail: pic@worldbank.org
Telephone: 202-458-5454
Facsimile: 202-522-1500

Independent Evaluation Group
Knowledge Programs and Evaluation Capacity
Development (IEGKE)
E-mail: eline@worldbank.org
Telephone: 202-458-4497
Facsimile: 202-522-3125

 Printed on Recycled Paper

Contents

ACRONYMS AND ABBREVIATIONS

APL	Adaptable Program Loan
ARDE	Annual Review of Development Effectiveness
BEEPS	Business Environment and Enterprise Performance Survey
CAE	Country Assistance Evaluation
CAS	Country Assistance Strategy
CDD	Community-driven development
CFAA	Country Financial Accountability Assessment
CPIA	Country Policy and Institutional Assessment
DECRG	Development Economics Research Group
EBRD	European Bank for Reconstruction and Development
ED	Education
EMT	Energy and mining
ENV	Environment
EP	Economic policy
EU	European Union
FY	Fiscal year
GDP	Gross domestic product
GIC	Global information and communications
FSP	Financial sector policy
HIPC	Heavily Indebted Poor Countries (Initiative)
HNP	Health, nutrition, and population
IBRD	International Bank for Reconstruction and Development
ICR	Implementation Completion Report
ICRG	International Country Risk Guide
IDA	International Development Association
IEG	Independent Evaluation Group
IFPRI	International Food Policy Research Institute
KDP	Kecamatan Development Project
KKM	Kaufmann, Kraay, Mastruzzi
LICUS	Low-Income Country Under Stress
LIL	Lending and Innovation Loan
MDG	Millennium Development Goal
NGO	Nongovernmental organization
OECD	Organisation for Economic Co-operation and Development
OED	Operations Evaluation Department (renamed IEG, December 2005)
PETS	Public Expenditure Tracking Survey
PIU	Project Implementation Unit
PMU	Project Monitoring Unit
PPAR	Project Performance Assessment Report
PPP	Purchasing power parity
PREM	Poverty Reduction and Economic Management Network (World Bank)

PRSC	Poverty Reduction Support Credit
PRSP	Poverty Reduction Strategy Paper
PSAL	Programmatic Structural Adjustment Loan
PSD	Private sector development
PSG	Public sector and governance
QAG	Quality Assurance Group (World Bank)
RDV	Rural development
SP	Social protection
SWAp	Sectorwide approach
TI	Transparency International
TR	Transportation
UD	Urban development
USAID	United States Agency for International Development
WDI	World Development Indicators
WDR	World Development Report
WSS	Water supply and sanitation
WUA	Water users association

OED changed its name to Independent Evaluation Group in December 2005.

Acknowledgments

This review was prepared by a team led by Monika Huppi. The core team comprised Shonar Lala, Mirafe Marcos, and Rupa Ranganathan. Shalini Ishwar Ahuja, Patricia Y. Chen, and Nara Meli provided research assistance. William B. Hurlbut and Caroline McEuen edited the report. Yezena Yimer assisted in the production of the report and Julia Akumu Ooro provided administrative support.

Contributions from numerous Independent Evaluation Group (IEG) staff are gratefully acknowledged. In addition, helpful comments were received from the following Bank staff: Surendra Agarwal, Ian Bannon, Deepak Bhattasali, Francois Bourguignon, Louise Cord, Aline Coudouel, Sebastian Dessus, Shantayanan Devarajan, Brigitte Duces, Shahrokh Fardoust, Marianne Fay, Ariel Fiszbein, Faezeh Foroutan, Alan Gelb, Philippe Le Houerou, Homi Kharas, Stephen Knack, Gregory Kisunko, Stefan Koeberle, Frannie Leautier, Luc Lecuit, Danny Leipziger, Richard Messick, Gisu Mohadjer, Julia Nielson, Aloysius Uche Ordu, Praful Patel, Patti Petesch, Philip Schuler, Sándor Sipos, James Stevens, Eric Swanson, Richard Tobin, John Underwood, Roberto Zagha, and Sally Zeijlon.

Assistance by Shaohua Chen, Prem Sangraula, and Kathleen Beegle with the calculation of poverty measures based on the Development Research Group's Povcalnet database is gratefully acknowledged.

Peer review was provided by Carol Lancaster and Manuel Penalver-Quesada.

The review was prepared under the direction of Victoria Elliott, Manager of IEG, Corporate Evaluation and Methods.

Director-General, Evaluation: *Vinod Thomas*
Director, Independent Evaluation Group–World Bank: *Ajay Chhibber*
Manager, Corporate Evaluation and Methods: *Victoria Elliott*
Task Manager: *Monika Huppi*

Foreword

The aim of the World Bank's results agenda is to design country assistance programs and development projects that go beyond delivering assistance, to ensuring poverty reduction in socially and environmentally sustainable ways. Effective and sustained reductions in poverty result from a combination of sustained economic growth, policies and investments that improve income distribution, and the delivery of services to the poor. Achieving this combination of outcomes, in turn, requires capable public institutions that are accountable to their stakeholders for the results they achieve.

This *Annual Review of Development Effectiveness* (ARDE) assembles evidence from the recent work of the Independent Evaluation Group of the World Bank to explore the record of countries and the Bank in helping achieve results along the poverty reduction results chain. It looks at three core questions. First, how efficiently has growth translated into poverty reduction in Bank-assisted countries, and what factors have contributed to the effectiveness of Bank assistance toward achieving this result? Second, what factors help interventions lead to high-quality development results in sectors that deliver services to the poor? Third, what types of Bank assistance have helped raise the accountability of public institutions in charge of delivering and sustaining results?

The review identifies three important determinants of the Bank's effectiveness in helping countries reduce poverty. First, it is important to understand the nature of growth and to identify the binding constraints to growth that creates jobs and reaches regions where many of the poor are concentrated. It is also important to identify factors that hinder intersectoral mobility of the poor. Second, the results chain is a valuable but underused tool that can help ensure that objectives are realistic and that the crucial cross-sectoral constraints to their achievement are considered. Finally, a realistic assessment of the political economy of governance-related reforms increases the effectiveness of interventions aimed at strengthening the accountability of public sector institutions.

Vinod Thomas
Director-General, Evaluation

Executive Summary

A results-based approach to development tracks the contributions to progress in reducing poverty, going beyond questions concerning the delivery of development assistance. Effective and sustained reductions in poverty, the evidence shows, result from a combination of sustained economic growth and policies and investments that affect income distribution and the delivery of services to the poor. Achieving this combination of outcomes requires capable public institutions that are accountable to their stakeholders for the results they achieve.

This *Annual Review of Development Effectiveness* (ARDE) brings together evaluative evidence from the recent work of the Independent Evaluation Group of the World Bank to address three questions surrounding this results chain in countries, with a particular focus on the Bank's role in the chain:

- How effectively has economic growth translated into poverty reduction in Bank-assisted countries, and what factors have affected these results?
- What factors have led to high-quality results in areas that deliver services to the poor?
- What measures help raise the accountability of public institutions responsible for delivering and sustaining results?

The report identifies features that characterize the country experiences and assistance programs that have delivered results:

- Effective programs have a twofold focus: they emphasize both the ingredients of growth and the measures that help the poor share in the growth process.
- They build on a realistic and well-informed assessment of the political commitment and capacity of the recipient to deliver results, and they emphasize coalition and capacity building to help attain results.
- They combine sustained engagement with clear intermediate milestones.
- Finally, they emphasize improved transparency and local control of public institutions, factors that spur these institutions to deliver results.

Some Growth Patterns Reduce Poverty More Effectively than Others

Economic growth over the past decade has led to substantial poverty reduction in many East and South Asian countries, and more recently in the transition economies of Eastern Europe and

Central Asia. Impressive advances in the world's most populous countries, China and India, have been at the forefront of the reduction in global poverty. This progress notwithstanding, poverty reduction remains a formidable challenge for many Bank borrowers.

The growth performance of World Bank borrowers has strengthened over the past five years, but achieving the sustained income growth essential to poverty reduction remains a challenge for many. Only 2 in 5 borrowing countries recorded continuous per capita income growth during the 5 years between 2000 and 2005, and just 1 in 5 did so for the full 10 years from 1995 to 2005.

Countries that have posted strong growth have exhibited better policies and institutions than slow growers. The strongest growers have better records of both economic management and policies for social inclusion than do moderate or slow growers. This indicates that high growth can be achieved alongside policies for social inclusion.

High and sometimes worsening income inequality has dampened the poverty-reducing effect of growth in a number of countries. This effect was particularly noteworthy where growth was concentrated in sectors that generated little employment and where the poor lacked the basic skills or mobility to take advantage of the opportunities presented by growth. Growth delivers poverty reduction more effectively when it occurs in sectors and regions where most of the poor live and work and when it results in strong job creation.

Strategies designed solely to boost overall growth may miss opportunities to reduce poverty more effectively. In the countries reviewed by the Independent Evaluation Group (IEG) where growth did not result in poverty reduction, growth was concentrated in subsectors with low labor intensity and where few of the poor could work. The Bank's assistance in these countries often effectively contributed to bringing the countries back to a growth path through improved economic management, but

it was less successful in bringing about job-creating growth. In Madagascar, for example, the Bank's assistance strategy included putting the overextended public sector on firmer ground and establishing the preconditions for private sector growth. It focused on sectors with high growth potential that would allow for relatively quick payoffs, but their impact on poverty was limited. In Georgia, the oil transport sector was a major driver of growth, but it created little employment. The Bank Group's assistance helped reestablish macroeconomic stability and contributed to growth in the oil transport sector, but was less successful in helping to remove obstacles to more broad-based growth.

The Bank has found it challenging to help countries formulate and implement strategies that effectively reduce rural poverty. Half of the Country Assistance Strategy reviews completed by IEG over the past four fiscal years concluded that the Bank's assistance in rural areas had either not led to satisfactory outcomes or that rural poverty reduction required increased attention.

To support growth strategies that more consistently translate into poverty reduction, the Bank and its partners will need to further strengthen their understanding of what keeps the poor from participating in growth in each country, what prevents growth from reaching regions and sectors where the poor are concentrated, and how urban-rural linkages and intersectoral mobility can be enhanced.

Achieving Results Requires Setting Realistic Objectives

The Bank's assistance has been effective when it has taken a realistic view of borrowers' political and institutional capacity and has focused on well-specified objectives. But almost half of all Bank Country Assistance Strategies reviewed by IEG in the past four fiscal years were found to be overly ambitious in two distinct ways. They either lacked selectivity or they were founded on unrealistic expectations for a reform program that was incommensurate with the country's institutional capacity and political situation.

Strategies that lacked selectivity caused the Bank's programs to spread their resources too thinly across too many sectors, diminishing the impact of individual operations. Strategies based on unrealistic expectations for reform led the Bank to proceed with policy-based lending even when country conditions were not fully ready for the targeted reforms. Country Assistance Evaluations suggest that several factors can help determine ex-ante whether an assistance strategy is realistic or not, including the country's record with reform implementation and realization of the Bank's assistance program, judicious analysis of the country's political economy and implementation capacity, and clear identification of country risks.

Unrealistic objectives can also be found in individual lending operations. For instance, many financial sector loans in crisis countries have had unduly ambitious objectives, driven by an overestimate of the government's commitment to reform and a need to justify large loans. Realistic and well-defined objectives, in contrast, can produce results when stakeholders focus on them. The Bank's support for Bolivia's health sector, for example, focused for a decade on infant and maternal health services and contributed to marked improvements in health outcomes for poor mothers and children.

Achieving Sector-Level Impact Requires More than Satisfactory Project Outcomes

The performance of the Bank's portfolio has improved over the past five fiscal years, with over three-quarters of completed operations meeting their stated objectives. However, Country Assistance Evaluations show that satisfactory project outcomes alone do not ensure country sector impact. Careful selection and phasing of interventions; long-term engagement; and the complementarities of lending, analytical work, and policy dialogue are factors that lead to impact on the sector as a whole. Bank-financed operations have yielded good results when they have supported a country-formulated, broadly owned sector strategy with clear objectives, and when they have followed a distinct pathway designed to reach milestones that contributed to the achievement of the country's objectives for the sector.

Balancing Long-Term and Short-Term Objectives Improves Results

Achieving high-quality development results takes time, but pressure to show results quickly can divert attention from the quality of results. For instance, the Millennium Development Goal of ensuring universal completion of primary education by 2015 has spurred massive efforts to increase enrollments. These rapid increases are welcome, but in many countries they have come at the expense of attention to learning outcomes. In Uganda, for example, access to education has improved greatly, but there are now 94 children per classroom and 3 students have to share a single textbook. Yet the experiences of Ghana, India, and Uruguay have shown that it is possible to combine increased access with gradual gains in learning outcomes. This requires careful strategic planning and a strong commitment to focus on learning outcomes from the outset. However, only about one-third of operations in the primary education sector assessed by IEG explicitly aimed to improve learning outcomes.

In post-conflict countries, the pressure to show quick results is especially intense, but haste may lead to the neglect of the institution building that is vital for recovery. In Timor-Leste, for example, three community empowerment projects supported by the Bank financed impressive amounts of local infrastructure, but too little attention was given to the development of durable local institutions.[1]

A judicious combination of long-term objectives and interventions that yield quick and visible results has proved effective. For example, Bank assistance to the education sector in Ghana combined support for policy reforms with funding for school buildings, furnishings, and teaching materials over 15 years. This sustained approach has helped produce a stream of physical improvements that have helped garner support for reforms needed to expand access, while gradually improving learning outcomes.

The long time required to achieve many of the intended results underlines the importance of continuity of donor engagement and of defining what is feasible for a single operation to achieve. Frequent shifts in emphasis of Bank assistance risk reducing its effectiveness.

Strong Results Demand Attention to Cross-Sectoral Synergies

Achieving results in a given sector often requires that constraints in other sectors be identified and removed as well. In Bangladesh, for example, Bank support for female secondary schooling and rural electrification significantly contributed to reductions in child mortality, alongside health sector interventions.

The countries and the Bank need to pay more attention to such complementary effects. The impact of infrastructure investments financed by community development projects, for example, has often been diminished by lack of attention to inputs such as teachers, doctors, and medicines. Similarly, Bank-supported pension reforms have sometimes failed to achieve the desired results because not enough attention was given to ensuring that the complementary macroeconomic, financial, and institutional conditions were in place. The workings of the Bank's matrix management structure do not provide staff with enough incentives to work across sectoral boundaries and address cross-sectoral issues.

More attention also needs to be given to the impact of reforms on different income groups, because not all pro-growth policies are distributionally neutral. In the area of trade reform, for example, the Bank often failed to conduct sufficient analysis to inform its policy advice and lending about the employment and poverty effects of reforms. A full assessment of the distributional impact of proposed reforms in a country often requires analysis that reaches beyond the sector in which the reforms are carried out.

Even though achieving a particular sector goal may require a multisectoral approach, large multisector operations are not always an effective vehicle for achieving sectoral results. The sectoral impact of multisector operations has tended to be weaker than that of sector-specific operations, partly because multisector operations allow for less-intensive engagement of Bank sector teams with country line agencies. In the financial sector, for example, the outcome of loans overseen by the Bank financial sector departments was substantially better than that of financial sector components of multisector loans.

A combination of policy-based lending (which is often multisectoral) and sector-specific operations can deliver good results. In Armenia and Ghana, for example, the Bank effectively used development policy lending to support reforms in the education sector, while parallel investment projects helped build the systems and capacity to implement the reforms.

Perceived Governance Quality Has Not Yet Responded to Large-Scale Public Sector Reforms

Achieving and maintaining results requires public sector institutions that are accountable to stakeholders. Bank Country Assistance Strategies accordingly put substantial emphasis on strengthening performance and accountability in the public sector. The bulk of the Bank's support has taken the form of reform programs in public administration and public financial management.

This assistance has led to improvements in the quality of public sector management processes in some countries, but has not yet translated into improvements in the perceived quality of governance in most of these countries. Yet recent progress in perceived governance quality in some countries in Eastern and Central Europe shows that it is possible to make progress in a limited time when there is strong country commitment.

Evaluation suggests that public sector reform initiatives have not always been aligned with political circumstances. They have focused on new legislation and institutions, while overlooking enforcement. They have also tended to overlook the interface between the public and private sectors, even though regulatory reforms have often been found effective against corruption.

Civil Service Reforms Require Political Commitment

Public sector reforms of a technocratic nature, such as modernizing personnel practices, can succeed when they build on political commitment. Bulgaria's achievement in professionalizing its civil service, for instance, has been the product of both donor-supported reforms in pay and recruitment and broad political interest in meeting conditions for European Union (EU) accession. But many reform programs have been undermined by lack of political support. The extent of political opposition is often underestimated at the time of design. In Bolivia and Yemen, Bank-supported reforms in civil service management achieved little, because there was no commitment to ending the traditional role of the public service as a vehicle for large-scale patronage appointments. When political conditions are not ready for wholesale reforms, it is advisable to proceed gradually, identifying opportunities for less-contentious reforms in order to build coalitions across affected interests and to gradually gain momentum.

Anticorruption Measures Need Enforcement Mechanisms

The Bank's anticorruption efforts have helped support new laws and institutions in many countries. But once established, they have often proved ineffective because they lack enforcement capacity. Anticorruption agencies, while important, have only a limited impact on the prevalence of corruption when they are not fully independent of those whose behavior they monitor.

The need for enforcement capacity to properly implement legislation to improve transparency and accountability reaches beyond anticorruption efforts. The implementation of prudential regulations and supervision in the banking sector has also suffered from low enforcement

capacity. Typically, Bank assistance programs have emphasized legal and regulatory frameworks for the financial sector, but they have underestimated the time and human capacity required to enforce them.

Regulatory Reform Helps Beat Corruption

The interface between the private and public sectors offers fertile ground both for corruption and for combating it. Reforms to regulatory regimes have made headway against corruption even when they have not been part of comprehensive anticorruption programs. In Turkey, for example, a Bank program for the energy sector supported the establishment of an independent regulatory agency that enabled sellers and buyers of electricity to make contracts directly, without involving government officials. It thereby sharply limited the opportunities for officials to seek kickbacks. Such sector-specific opportunities to combat corruption need to be more systematically exploited in Bank operations.

Transparency and Local Control Encourage the Public Sector to Deliver

Transparency is the foundation of good governance, because access to information reduces the incidence of corruption, and transparent institutions earn the public's trust. Bank operations have helped bring more transparency to a variety of public management processes, including budget formulation and execution, procurement, and customs administration. In the Philippines and Uganda, for example, the Bank has worked with governments to make the public procurement process more transparent. Civil society representatives have a mandate to observe the tendering process in the Philippines, while Uganda makes its final contract awards and related tendering information available on public Web sites.

Local control and community participation can make public sector institutions more accountable. Bank operations support such local control in two main ways: by up-grading local government agencies and by channeling resources directly to communities through community-driven development projects. Such projects have often established structures that parallel those of local government, which has diluted efforts to foster decentralization.[2] In Jamaica, for instance, roads were built under community development operations without adequate involvement of the local councils that would have to maintain them. There is now growing recognition in the Bank of the importance of strengthening the use of local systems while promoting community development.[3]

Going Forward

This ARDE finds three important areas where the Bank can further strengthen its effectiveness in helping countries reduce poverty:

- *A focus on the nature of growth:* Poverty reduction will continue to require a strong focus on growth. To ensure that growth translates efficiently into poverty reduction, the countries, the Bank, and their partners will need to focus more on finding effective ways of helping the poor participate in this growth. This will require country-level analysis of the binding constraints to employment-creating growth and to growth in regions where many of the poor live, as well as of the factors that hinder intersectoral mobility of the poor.

- *A clearly articulated results chain:* A well-articulated results chain allows Bank operations to ensure that objectives are realistic, that cross-sectoral constraints to achieving them are adequately considered, and that due attention is given to capacity building. Effective articulation and utilization of the results chain also requires efforts to enhance country capacity to collect and use performance information.

- *A realistic assessment of the political economy of governance-related reforms:* The Bank can provide countries with the tools needed to strengthen government processes, and thereby to improve the governance environment, but effective use of those tools remains in the hands of country decision makers. Thus, reforms to improve the accountability of public sector institutions require broad-based political support. When such support is absent, an incremental approach that allows momentum for reforms to build can help deliver results. These reforms can be further enhanced with continued efforts to foster local demand for accountability through increased transparency of government processes and resource utilization.

Management Comments: Summary

We very much value the 2006 *Annual Review of Development Effectiveness* (ARDE) as part of the strong tradition of evaluation in the World Bank. Decision making within Bank management is made with the benefit of feedback from the Independent Evaluation Group (IEG), as well as from the Bank's internal Quality Assurance Group (QAG). Management prepared detailed comments on the 2006 ARDE as part of the background for discussions with executive directors (first at the Board's Committee on Development Effectiveness, and later at an informal meeting of executive directors). This note summarizes some of the main points of management's comments, highlighting recent actions.

Developing Country Growth. The ARDE paints an overly bleak picture of developing country growth and poverty reduction, failing to fully reflect both strong global growth trends over the last five years and broadly favorable prospects. Developing countries grew at 5–6 percent between 2004 and 2006, even excluding fast-growing China and India. This year the number is expected to be 6.8 percent—a fifth strong year of growth. Low-income developing countries have done especially well, with high average annual income growth (more than 6½ percent) over five years. Sub-Saharan Africa has not been left out of this positive trend. Average annual growth there in the last five years is 4.7 percent. Over the past decade, two-thirds of Africans have lived in countries with a 5 percent or higher average growth rate. This is an amazing performance, given the challenges on the continent, including HIV/AIDS, a high incidence of conflict-affected countries, and, more recently, high oil prices. These impressive growth rates reflect the strong policy performance of developing countries, including in Africa (as noted in the 2003 ARDE and as has continued since then). While management applauds their efforts, it knows that the World Bank must do more still to help countries to reinforce and accelerate this trend.

Operational Quality. Management notes with satisfaction the continued improvement in the performance of Bank-supported projects. The ARDE reports that for the cohort of operations completed in fiscal 2005 and evaluated so far, development outcomes were rated as satisfactory in 82 percent of operations (87 percent when weighted by disbursements), sustaining a long-term upward trend in quality. These strong results have been achieved with higher lending from the International Bank for Reconstruction and Development and increased credits and grants from the International Development Association (IDA). In fiscal 2006, IDA provided a record $9.5 billion in support to poor countries, with more than half going to Sub-Saharan Africa. IDA financing reflects a performance-based allocation system that rewards, and thus encourages, recipient countries' effective use of funds for development and poverty reduction.

Successful Country Assistance Strategies (CASs). The issues raised in the ARDE with respect to CASs, selectivity, and cross-sectoral synergies are not new. Indeed, they reinforce management's determination to continue with its accelerated results agenda, and in particular to continue with its recently introduced results-based CAS program (see World Bank 2006a). (Management would note that much of the analysis in the ARDE is based on outcomes of strategies, which raises a major question regarding attribution: clearly, as the ARDE states, the Bank cannot take credit when poverty outcomes are good; but the reverse is also true. Moreover, the ARDE does not say much on donor harmonization and alignment—important management objectives with the goal of improving the quality of overall donor assistance to countries.)

Distributional Impacts. Management takes the issue of the distributional impact of growth seriously. That is the reason it has worked with other donors to pilot and mainstream Poverty and Social Impact Assessments and has revised its policy on development policy lending to take into account possible adverse poverty and social impacts and, as necessary, to include measures to mitigate them. Operationalizing the recent

World Development Report (WDR), *Equity and Development* (World Bank 2005k), is under way and will reinforce attention to pro-poor growth.

The Challenge of Rural Poverty. Management shares IEG's concerns with respect to rural poverty and has taken action in this area. Since the adoption in 2003 of the Bank's new rural strategy (World Bank 2003a), the Bank's rural staff report that CASs are stronger on rural poverty, and, more important, country-owned poverty reduction strategies now include rural poverty diagnoses. Lending for rural development is up; in fiscal 2006 it accounted for 14 percent of total lending commitments. IEG and QAG data show improvements in the quality of Bank-supported rural projects. The 2007 WDR currently under preparation will help hone further our knowledge on how best to support rural and agricultural development. It will provide more clarity on customizing agricultural strategies to specific country conditions and on dealing with the risks posed by heavy and often unpredictable government intervention in agricultural export markets.

Governance Issues. Management agrees with much of the ARDE's analysis on civil service reform, transparency, and anticorruption. That is why more recent operational support has focused on service-oriented approaches to improving governance and service provision. Management has also worked with development partners to devise and implement a public financial management performance measurement framework that is more objective than previous perception measures (see World Bank 2005g). Early experience with the tool is encouraging. Management recently took the initiative to strengthen its strategy for Bank Group engagement on governance and anticorruption. Consultations with partners are currently taking place, and management will be reviewing progress regularly with executive directors as the strategy is further refined.

Chairman's Summary: Committee on Development Effectiveness (CODE)

On October 18, 2006, the Committee on Development Effectiveness discussed the *Annual Review of Development Effectiveness 2006: Getting Results* (ARDE) and the *Draft Management Response.*

2006 ARDE

Building on the 2004 ARDE that examined the Bank's contribution to poverty reduction, the 2006 ARDE considered the factors at the country, sector, and institutional levels that facilitate or hinder poverty-reducing growth and effective service delivery to the poor, and how the Bank has taken these elements into account in its operations. Drawing on recent IEG evaluations of World Bank operations, the 2006 ARDE considered: (1) how efficiently economic growth has translated into poverty reduction, and what factors contributed to the effectiveness of Bank support towards achieving these results; (2) what factors have helped interventions lead to high-quality development results in sectors that deliver services to the poor; and (3) what types of Bank assistance have helped increase the accountability of public institutions responsible for delivering and sustaining results. The Annual Review identified three key areas where the Bank can further strengthen its

effectiveness: focus on the nature of growth to ensure that the poor can benefit from economic growth; clearly articulate the results chain to ensure that objectives are set realistically and that key cross-sectoral constraints to achieving them are adequately identified and addressed; and build on a realistic assessment of the political economy of governance-related reforms.

Draft Management Response

Management found many of IEG's findings and recommendations useful as inputs into improving the development impact of Bank support. At the same time, it noted that the Annual Review portrays a pessimistic view on growth and poverty reduction. Management also suggested that the ARDE could have been more balanced, to reflect the current Bank approach to country assistance strategies, the difficulties around strategy development in uncertain environments, the achievements in terms of continuing improvements in quality at entry and exit of operations with a growing volume of lending, and the focus on service-oriented approaches to improving governance and service delivery, and recent work to strengthen engagement with client countries on governance.

Overall Conclusions and Next Steps

The Committee appreciated the candid report and welcomed the findings on the sustained improvements in project quality, although much remained to be done. Indeed, many members felt that management need not be defensive or embarrassed about the results and should maintain a positive approach to learning from experience.

Members discussed the strategic issue of quality of economic growth for poverty reduction, and the ARDE observations related to potentials of growth resulting in job creation and productivity for the poor, and the challenges of rural poverty reduction. There was general support for ARDE's call for setting more realistic objectives in country assistance strategies, as well as in individual operations. In this regard, members highlighted the importance of solid analytical work (including political economy) and the involvement of local institutions and experts in this area; the need to balance short- and long-term objectives; and the effective use of the results chain to set realistic objectives and identify sectoral and cross-sectoral constraints to reach the stated objectives. Members supported addressing cross-sectoral constraints for strong sector results, including the issue of matrix management structure and organizational incentives to support work across sectors. The chapter on public sector accountability drew interest in the context of the Bank's new governance and anti-corruption strategy. Some speakers noted that the ARDE could have incorporated gender dimensions and aspects of harmonization.

The main issues raised during the meeting were the following:

ARDE's Findings. The Committee appreciated the candid report, although a few members echoed management's view that the ARDE presented an overly pessimistic perspective of countries' performances in reducing poverty, and it could have presented a more balanced picture of the Bank's contributions. One member felt that the ARDE's objectives were ambitious and it may have presented a simplified picture of the complex development issues. A number of speakers indicated it could have further differentiated between the poor, in particular to take into account the gender dimensions. *IEG pointed to a number of country sector examples in the ARDE that illustrate how gender issues were addressed. It also indicated willingness to undertake another review of gender, which had last been evaluated in 2000. Management reminded the Committee of the Gender Action Plan, and the forthcoming Global Monitoring Report will also cover gender issues.* The tendency to group African countries together and then generalize the findings, which were too broad, was also noted. Several speakers suggested the report might have better defined the methodology, terms, and data used, regarding which there were a number of comments and questions.

Focus on Quality of Growth. The ARDE finding that growth more effectively reduced poverty when it occurred in regions where most of the poor live and in job-creating sectors resonated with a number of speakers. However, some speakers cautioned against focusing too narrowly on job-creating sectors or "cherry picking," and noted the need to address broader development issues that may be more challenging to address. Some members supported more attention to job creation for the poor, and observed that the ARDE could have elaborated on the role of the private sector in creating jobs, and on contributions of International Finance Corporation (IFC) and World Bank Group synergies in this area. *IEG noted that ARDE covered the World Bank activities, while IEG-IFC prepares a separate review of IFC activities. It also indicated that it was looking at ways to review the World Bank Group synergies in its evaluation work.* Several speakers commented on the need to strengthen Bank support for rural development, taking into account the rural-urban linkages. One member sought information about the weaknesses and constraints of Bank assistance in rural development, while another asked about the Bank plans to improve outcomes. *Management viewed rural development as an important area for support, noted that the results of the new rural strategy cannot yet be measured, and also remarked on the need to address the overall trade environment.* Deepening country-specific knowledge of the constraints to the poor's participation in the benefits of growth and the distributional impact of growth-enhancing reforms was emphasized.

Selectivity and Setting Realistic Objectives. Generally, speakers supported ARDE's call for greater realism in country assistance strategies, as well as in individual operations. The results-based Country Assistance Strategies (CASs) were considered key to selectivity and setting realistic objectives. *Management broadly agreed, but it also echoed the view of a few speakers that optimism and ambition are also needed in development.*

- ***Country analytical work:*** Speakers stressed solid country analytical work (including political economy) to underpin country strategies and to support greater selectivity and proper sequencing of Bank assistance, especially in Low-Income Countries Under Stress/fragile states. Some speakers urged more involvement of local institutions and experts to promote country ownership. *Management remarked on its increased efforts to consider the political context and country ownership issues.* In order to be effective, members emphasized the need to strengthen country capacity for data collection and analyses, and for monitoring and evaluation. A few remarked on the importance of integrating technical assistance for capacity building in the overall assistance strategy.

- ***Short- and Long- Term Objectives:*** The need to balance short- and long- term objectives and the importance of sequencing, especially when countries face capacity issues and/or political resistance, was noted. In this

connection, speakers supported a better-articulated and more realistic results chain. *Management assured the Committee that it is using a results chain, which is a central element of the Results-Based CAS. It also expected that the increased emphasis on impact analysis would also help strengthen the results chain.*

- ***Policy-Based Lending:*** A member considered realistic country assessment critical for policy-based lending and sought to ensure staff incentives and support in this area. Another member urged closer monitoring of the implementation and results of policy-based lending. *Management noted that the bulk of the Bank's development policy support has gone to countries with higher Country Policy and Institutional Assessment (CPIA) ratings, indicating a better policy and institutional environment.*

Enhancing Sectoral Impacts through Cross-Sectoral Synergies. The Committee concurred with the need to overcome cross-sectoral constraints for strong sector results, which *IEG elaborated on, referring to a number of examples.* Two members noted the transaction costs associated with coordination and implementation, and the need to work across line agencies at the country level. Of particular concern to most speakers were the constraints posed by the matrix management structure and staff incentives to work across sectors, and management action in this area. Different views were expressed in response to a member's question as to whether cross-sectoral work was limited by the organizational structure or by lack of appropriate incentives. *Management did not consider structure as the main underlying issue limiting work across sectors. It commented on the need for behavioral changes, observing that limited cross-sectoral work may also be attributed to the Bank hiring professionals with strong sector skills.*

Strengthening Public Sector Accountability. Speakers stressed the importance of country ownership, broad-based support, political commitment, and the long-term perspective needed in improving governance, which were highlighted in the ARDE. In this context, one member cautioned about Bank's involvement in coalition building when political conditions were not ready for broad-based public sector reform. *IEG clarified that better results have been associated with an incremental approach to public sector reform, taking into account the country's political situation to allow governments to align support for its reforms.* Other speakers stressed the importance of working with local governments in community-driven development initiatives. *Both management and IEG remarked that more recent community-driven development operations are taking into account the need to work closely with local governments.*

The unchanged perceptions of governance quality at the country level, despite the implementation of Bank-supported public sector reforms, were of concern to some speakers. Some speakers questioned the usefulness of the governance indicators, and one member urged extra care in the underlying methodology of the CPIA and World Bank Institute governance indicators. A few speakers expressed interest in the factors that support societal and attitudinal changes, for which one member proposed establishing process indicators. Responding to a question about the record

of public financial management in the Africa Region, *management said that the actual results for public administration reform had been mixed, while that of public expenditure and financial management was stronger*. A member supported ARDE's point that sector initiatives having a positive impact on governance should be further encouraged, even when they are not labeled as "governance support."

Harmonization and Coordination. Several speakers referred to the limited Bank resources, the need for the Bank to complement other donors' efforts, and the importance of donor coordination and harmonization. Some suggested ARDE could have considered whether harmonization, in line with the Paris Declaration on Aid Effectiveness, led to better overall results at the country level. *IEG recognized the importance of reviewing the extent to which harmonization is contributing to better results. It emphasized that such a review should be done jointly with other partners, which is a challenge. IEG mentioned that a joint evaluation of donor harmonization efforts is being contemplated under the auspices of the OECD/DAC. Management mentioned it was preparing a report on harmonization and aid effectiveness, which will soon be considered by the Board.*

Pietro Veglio, Chairman

Introduction

The desire to strengthen the effectiveness of development assistance and to demonstrate results has intensified over the past several years. High-level international meetings, such as the Monterrey Forum on Harmonization, the Marrakech Roundtable on Managing for Development Results, and the Paris Forum on Aid Effectiveness have highlighted the need to shift from a focus on development inputs to the achievement of verified outcomes.

The World Bank's way of measuring its operational performance has also evolved, reflecting this shift in the external environment. In the early 1990s, tracking of the number of projects and lending amounts was supplemented by a focus on improving the quality of Bank operations. Attention has turned more recently toward the achievement of results as an indicator of the Bank's effectiveness. In parallel, the Bank's lending has shifted from lending mainly for physical investments toward more emphasis on strengthening the quality of institutions as a core ingredient to achieving high-impact results.

Development assistance is only effective if it produces results that have a positive impact. Substantial effort has gone into setting targets and developing indicators to monitor progress toward achieving results within the agenda of the Millennium Development Goals (MDGs), in the framework of IDA14 (International Development Association, fourteenth replenishment), and more recently for the Bank's corporate sector strategies. But availability of credible information needed to monitor progress toward results, and ultimately to measure the development impact of particular interventions, remains a formidable challenge in many client countries. Efforts to help countries build capacity to generate, analyze, and use data for decision making and policy formulation have been stepped up to support the results agenda. These efforts remain a work in progress.

Despite the challenges of measurement, evidence is emerging from project, country, sector, and thematic evaluations about the factors that increase the likelihood of achieving meaningful results. Drawing on this evidence, the *2006 Annual Review of Development Effectiveness* (ARDE) examines the effectiveness of Bank support in helping countries achieve high-impact results. Like previous ARDEs, this report draws primarily on Independent Evaluation Group (IEG) evaluation findings for Bank programs and projects.

The 2002 ARDE, *Achieving Development Outcomes: The Millennium Challenge*, found that while the MDGs can help sharpen the development effort by focusing achievement on quantified and time-bound development targets, they also pose an inherent risk of nonattainment. The 2004 ARDE, *The World Bank's Contribution to Poverty Reduction*, found that linking the Bank's country-level interventions to poverty reduction requires a sharper results focus. This year's ARDE builds on these findings by looking at what factors facilitate or hinder the achievement of high-impact results at the country, sector, and institutional levels and how the Bank has taken those factors into consideration.

The World Bank's overarching objective is to help countries reduce poverty in socially and environmentally sustainable ways. To achieve this objective, countries must attain sustained growth and ensure that such growth effectively translates into poverty reduction. Poverty reduction also requires that the poor be able to avail themselves of services that equip them to take advantage of the opportunities arising from growth. Achieving poverty-reducing growth and effective service delivery requires capable public sector institutions that are accountable to stakeholders for the results they achieve. Against this backdrop, the ARDE considers three questions:

- How efficiently has growth in countries assisted by the Bank translated into poverty reduction, and what factors have contributed to the effectiveness of Bank assistance toward achieving this result?
- What factors help interventions lead to high-quality development results, particularly in sectors that deliver services to the poor?
- What kinds of Bank assistance have helped raise the accountability of public institutions in charge of delivering and sustaining results?

Chapter 2: Evaluation Highlights

- Achieving poverty reduction remains a substantial challenge because growth has remained uneven and sporadic and has translated into poverty reduction with varying efficiency.
- Strategies for poverty reduction need to consider where the poor live and how they earn income.
- Strengthening urban-rural linkages and strategies to improve rural productivity requires more attention.
- The distributional effects of growth-enhancing reforms need to receive more attention.
- Assistance strategies have been effective when they have taken political and institutional capacity into account. When they have not done so, they have been overly ambitious and lacked focus.

Achieving Poverty-Reducing Growth

When focusing on results at the country level, the World Bank's overarching objective is poverty reduction. Economic growth is essential for poverty reduction, yet all growth is not equal in improving the welfare of the poor. Effective poverty reduction also requires that low-income groups be able to participate in economic growth.

This chapter reviews how well countries assisted by the Bank have fared in achieving poverty-reducing growth and examines the factors contributing to Bank effectiveness in getting this result. The chapter draws on IEG Country Assistance Evaluations completed in fiscal 2003–06, as well as IEG analyses of Country Assistance Strategy Completion Reports from fiscal 2004–06, for a total of 48 countries. It also uses poverty data available from the Bank's Povcalnet database over the periods covered by the IEG evaluations. Such information is available for 25 of the 48 countries. The chapter will refer to the group of 48 countries as the *full sample* and the group of 25 countries as the *subsample*.

Economic Growth—the Recent Record

Growth in the majority of Bank borrowers has been stronger in the most recent five years than in the first half of the decade from 1995 to 2005 (figure 2.1). Nevertheless, achievement of sustained increases in per capita income, essential for poverty reduction, continues to elude a considerable number of countries. The aggregate picture of growth and income in client countries over the past decade has three main characteristics:

- ***Middle-income countries were more likely to grow than low-income countries.*** Almost 90 percent of middle-income countries achieved a positive annual per capita income growth rate during 1995–2005, and about three-quarters of low-income countries did so (figure 2.2).
- ***There are still many slow growers.*** Only two of five countries were able to increase per capita income at an average annual rate of 2.5 percent or better during 1995–2005, and one in seven countries had a negative average annual per capita income growth rate during this time (figure 2.2).
- ***Among countries that did grow, sustaining growth was a challenge.*** Only 2 of 5 countries recorded continuous per capita income growth during 2000–05, and just 1 in 5 did so for a full 10 years from 1995 to 2005.

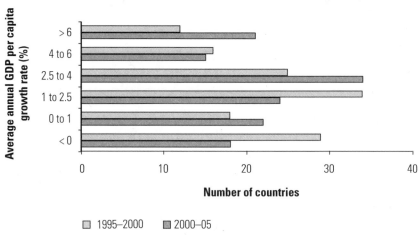

Figure 2.1: Growth Performance Has Improved, but Sustained Income Growth Remains a Challenge for Many Bank Borrowers

Source: World Bank 2006n.

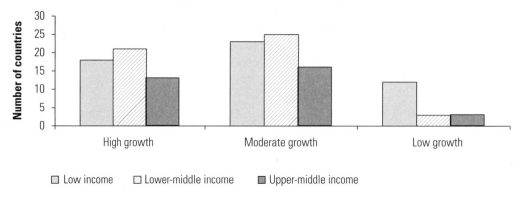

Figure 2.2: Middle-Income Countries Were More Likely to Experience Strong Growth than Low-Income Countries (1995–2005)

Source: World Bank 2006n.

Note: High growth = average annual per capita GDP growth rate of > 2.5 percent; moderate growth = average annual per capita GDP growth of 0 –2.5 percent; low growth = average annual per capita GDP growth < 0 percent.

High-growth countries have stronger policies and institutions than countries with slower growth.

Sustained and sustainable growth is the result of multiple interlinked factors, including a country's stock of physical, human, and environmental capital and the efficiency with which it is formed and used. Efficient capital formation, in turn, depends on the quality of macroeconomic, structural, social, and environmental policies and institutions.

The overall quality of policies and institutions (as measured by the Country Policy and Institutional Assessment, or CPIA, score) has been stronger in moderate- and high-growth countries than in low-growth countries. The performance gap of the slower-growth countries is most acute in their quality of economic management. High-

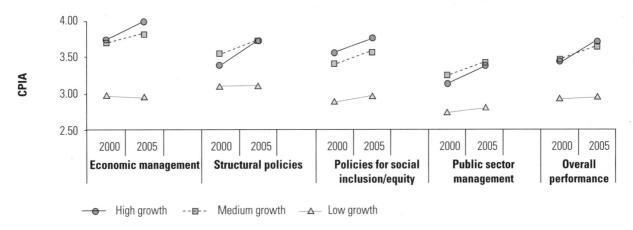

Figure 2.3: Countries with Higher Growth Have Stronger Economic Management and Better Policies for Social Inclusion and Equity than Slow Growers

Source: World Bank CPIA database.

Note: CPIA = Country Policy and Institutional Assessment.

growth countries also have stronger policies for social inclusion than moderate- and low-growth countries (figure 2.3), which demonstrates that high growth can be achieved alongside policies for social inclusion.

How Quality Growth Delivers Poverty Reduction

How effectively economic growth leads to the reduction of income poverty depends on how much the poor participate in growth. Increases in income and decreases in inequality can both lead to poverty reduction. The efficiency with which economic growth translates into poverty reduction depends on three factors: the initial level of income, initial inequality, and whether growth is accompanied by changes in inequality or not (Bourguignon 2004a, 2004b; Lopez and Serven 2006; Ravallion 1997, 2004; World Bank 2005f).[1] Specifically:

- A lower-income country will need to grow faster to achieve the same poverty reduction as a higher-income country with the same inequality level.
- A country with high inequality will need to grow faster than a country with a more equal income distribution to achieve the same poverty reduction.

- An increase in inequality will lower the poverty-reducing effect of growth.
- Poverty in richer and more unequal countries responds more strongly to changes in inequality than to changes in income.
- Poverty in poorer and more equal countries responds more strongly to changes in income than to changes in inequality.

Cross-country regression suggests that for a given level of income and inequality, growth translates more efficiently into poverty reduction in countries with high literacy rates, low regulatory burdens, and broad access to credit for the private sector (Chhibber and Nayyar 2006).

The extent to which growth reduces poverty is influenced by the initial levels of income and inequality and the pattern of growth.

Higher literacy facilitates poverty reduction because it increases the share of the population that can take advantage of better employment opportunities created by growth, while at the same time providing entrepreneurs with a lar-ger pool of skilled labor. Broad access to credit and a lower regulatory burden can facilitate entrepreneurial investment, which in turn

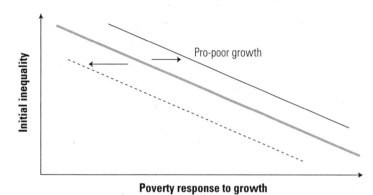

Figure 2.4: Policies and Investments that Enhance Equity Strengthen the Growth Effect on Poverty

Pro-poor growth

Initial inequality

Poverty response to growth

Source: Based on Chhibber and Nayyar 2006.

Policies and investments that take these factors into consideration can help enhance the efficiency with which growth reduces poverty (figure 2.4). The extent to which each of these factors constrains the ability of low-income groups to participate in growth depends on country-specific conditions, and thus calls for country-level analysis to help guide the formulation of growth strategies that translate efficiently into poverty reduction.

Reduction of Income Poverty in Bank-Assisted Countries

The share of people living on less than one dollar a day declined from 28 percent to 19 percent between 1990 and 2002 (World Bank 2006n). The global reduction in the number of poor people has been driven by impressive advances in East and South Asia, particularly China and India (box 2.1).[2]

helps create employment. Access to credit can also help low-income groups hedge against risk.

Other factors found to increase the efficiency of growth in reducing poverty are investments that increase the poor's access to infrastructure, measures that ensure market access for rural producers, investments in productivity-increasing agricultural technologies, and labor market regulations that create attractive employment opportunities for poor workers (World Bank 2005f).

To see how well Bank-assisted countries have fared in achieving poverty-reducing growth since the mid-1990s and how effectively Bank assistance has contributed to this result, we use the *subsample* of 25 Bank-assisted countries for which IEG has recently assessed the outcome of the Bank's country assistance and for which comparable poverty data are available from Povcalnet for at least two periods between the mid-1990s and the early 2000s.[3]

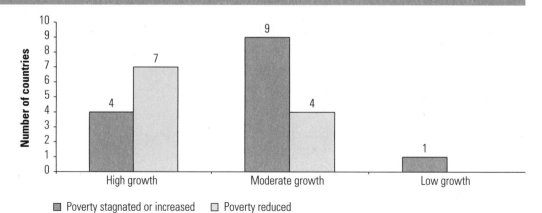

Figure 2.5: Poverty Reduction Remains a Significant Challenge, Even in Countries with Positive Growth Rates

■ Poverty stagnated or increased   □ Poverty reduced

Sources: Povcalnet, DECRG poverty database, World Bank 2006n.

Note: High growth = average annual per capita GDP growth rate of > 2.5 percent; moderate growth = average annual per capita GDP growth of 0–2.5 percent; low growth = average annual per capita GDP growth < 0 percent between survey years.

Box 2.1: China and India Account for a Large Share of the World's Poverty Reduction

The reduction in the absolute number of the world's poor has largely been driven by poverty reduction in the world's most populous countries, China and India.

China

No country has been more successful at reducing poverty in the past quarter-century than China. Between 1990 and 2005 alone, the number of people living on less than $2 a day fell by over 400 million. While migration to urban areas has helped reduce poverty nationally, the bulk of the poverty reduction through the mid-1990s came from within the rural areas, fuelled by policy reforms and technologies that increased productivity.

Since the late 1980s, however, an increase in vulnerability and inequality has dampened the poverty-reducing effect of growth. The Bank made several contributions to poverty reduction through its analytical and advisory services, poverty monitoring, and investments in agriculture, health, and transport. Most important, the Bank has helped establish successful models of targeted interventions through integrated rural development projects.

The Bank has been less successful in persuading the government of the implications of broader development policies for poverty and inequality. The mismatch between intergovernmental fiscal resources and responsibilities has exacerbated regional inequality, while migration restrictions have limited economic integration.

India

In India, there is broad agreement that poverty declined in the 1980s, although there is much dissent on the extent of poverty reduction in the 1990s. The official statistics indicate a 10-percentage-point drop in poverty—from 36 percent in 1993/94 to 26 percent in 1999/2000.

India's economy has performed impressively since the liberalization of trade and industrial policies in the early 1990s. This growth has enabled India to reduce poverty but has led to increasing income inequality that acts as a constraint to higher growth and stronger poverty reduction. The aggregate growth rate during the 1990s could have reduced poverty in India even more had growth been more balanced, sectorally and geographically. Poverty is increasingly concentrated in lagging regions where growth rates are substantially lower than in the rest of the country.

The Bank provided strong support for the reforms of the early 1990s. It expanded assistance to the social sectors and devoted more attention to improving participation. After the mid-1990s the Bank focused assistance on reforming states, with a notable measure of success. In the late 1990s, it sharpened its focus on poverty reduction and governance. Overall, however, the Bank had limited impact on fiscal and other structural reforms and failed to develop an effective assistance strategy for rural poverty reduction through much of the 1990s.

Sources: Datt and Ravallion 2002; Deaton and Kozel 2005; Devarajan and Nabi 2006; IEG 2001, 2005f; Ravallion and Chen 2004; World Bank 2006e.

Despite impressive advances in many East and South Asian countries over the past decade, poverty reduction remains a formidable challenge in many of the countries assisted by the Bank. Of the 25 countries in the subsample, only 11 reduced the incidence of poverty between the mid-1990s and the early 2000s, while poverty either stagnated or increased in the remaining 14 countries. Lackluster and volatile growth was a major reason for the limited poverty-reduction progress in the latter group (figures 2.5, 2.6).

Distributional changes are important for poverty reduction

Growth has been an important driver of poverty reduction in all of the sampled countries where poverty dropped. These countries experienced an average annual growth rate in per capita gross domestic product (GDP) of 2.5 percent or higher, except for Brazil. But in some countries growth did not efficiently translate into poverty reduction, because growth and changes in distribution did not work in the same direction (figure 2.7).

Poverty reduction remains a formidable challenge in many of the countries assisted by the Bank.

In the recovering transition economies of Armenia, Moldova, and Ukraine and in African countries that saw substantial poverty reduction, the poverty-reducing effect of growth was reinforced by a reduction in inequality. By contrast, in China, Lithuania, Sri Lanka, and Romania and in several Latin American

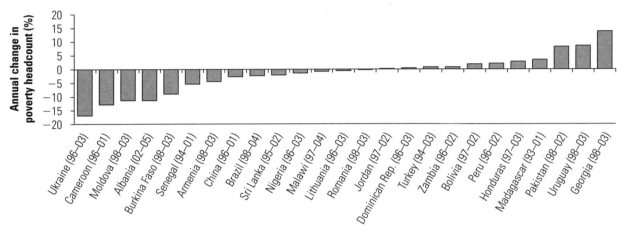

Figure 2.6: Of 25 Sampled Countries, 11 Witnessed Poverty Reduction Between the Mid-1990s and Early 2000s

Sources: Povcalnet, DECRG poverty database.

Note: Poverty changes based on per capita consumption/income and a poverty line of US$1.08/capita/ for low-income countries and US$2.15/capita/day (in 1993 purchasing power parity $) for middle-income countries and transition economies. Poverty figures may differ from country poverty estimates because of the use of different poverty lines and purchasing power parity exchange rates, as well as use of per capita rather than adult equivalent consumption.

countries, the positive effect of growth was dampened by worsening income distribution.

In some of the countries where poverty increased, such as Bolivia and Georgia, negative household consumption growth was accompanied by an increase in inequality. Brazil was an exception, because improvement in the income distribution translated into poverty reduction, despite the lack of income growth. While growth accounted for most of the poverty reduction across the sampled countries, even seemingly small changes in income distribution contributed substantially to either reinforcing or dampening the poverty effects of growth (appendix D).

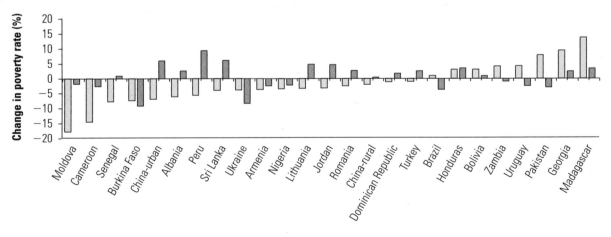

Figure 2.7: Changes in Distribution Reinforced the Poverty-Reducing Effect of Growth in Some Countries, but Dampened It in Others

☐ Change in poverty due to growth ■ Change in poverty due to change in distribution

Sources: Povcalnet, DECRG poverty database.

How Effectively Has World Bank Assistance Contributed to Poverty-Reducing Growth?[4]

To explore the correlation between the effectiveness of Bank assistance and poverty reduction, the subsample of 25 countries was divided into groups (table 2.1), depending on how well Bank assistance programs achieved their stated objectives. Not surprisingly, the successful outcome of a Country Assistance Strategy was correlated with the extent of poverty reduction achieved in a country, though this does not mean that poverty-reduction results can be attributed to Bank assistance alone. This assistance often represents only a small portion of the factors that influence overall country performance. Furthermore, while poverty reduction is the World Bank's overarching goal, individual Country Assistance Strategies set varying intermediate objectives toward contributing to this goal, and IEG evaluates the outcome against these strategy-specific objectives. This explains why the outcome of the Bank's assistance strategy was assessed as satisfactory by IEG in 40 percent of the subsampled countries that did not succeed in reducing poverty, while it was unsatisfactory in two countries where poverty was reduced (table 2.1).

Countries that reduced poverty and where the outcome of the Bank's assistance was satisfactory (countries in the upper-left quadrant of table 2.1) are distinguished from those with poor outcomes (lower-right quadrant) by substantially stronger economic management policies. Strong economic management helped spur growth, which translated into poverty reduction with varying efficiency. In these countries, the Bank supported government efforts to maintain—and at times reestablish—macroeconomic stability and fiscal discipline, including better targeting of public expenditures.

What makes for successful country assistance programs?

Three characteristics mark most of the assistance programs in the subsample countries where Bank assistance led to satisfactory results:

Growth was an important driver of poverty reduction, but even seemingly small changes in income distribution either dampened or reinforced the effects of growth on poverty.

- The country assistance programs were *selective* and in support of a government-owned program that the Bank had often supported through prior analytical work and policy dialogue.
- The pace of program implementation was *aligned with government capacity.*
- Assistance strategies were based on analytical work, often done in collaboration with local specialists, which helped *tailor* them *to country conditions.*

The experiences of Brazil, Burkina Faso, and China illustrate how important it is for the Bank's assistance program to be focused and tailored to country conditions. In Burkina Faso, the recently completed Country Assistance Strategy was closely aligned

Successful assistance programs were selective, aligned with government capacity, and tailored to country conditions.

Table 2.1: Country Assistance Outcomes and Poverty Changes (number of countries)

| | Country assistance outcome | |
Poverty change	Satisfactory/ moderately satisfactory	Moderately unsatisfactory/unsatisfactory
Poverty reduced	9	2
Poverty stagnated or increased	6	6

Source: Based on Country Assistance Evaluations and IEG analysis of Country Assistance Completion Reports.

Box 2.2: Burkina Faso—Focused Country Assistance Strategy with Measurable Milestones Yields Results

The Bank's Country Assistance Strategy (CAS) in Burkina Faso was closely aligned with the government's own strategy as outlined in the Poverty Reduction Strategy Paper (PRSP).

The Bank's interventions in support of the PRSP were deliberately selective and focused on well-specified objectives within each pillar of the government's program. Assistance combined support for policy reforms to strengthen the competitiveness of the economy, targeted public sector reforms, and specific poverty-targeted interventions designed to improve the access of the poor to public services and to increase rural productivity.

To assess its effectiveness, the CAS identified 14 monitorable indicators and specific monitoring instruments for each indicator. Progress was monitored against benchmarks, but IEG found that further progress could be made by closely tracking intermediate indicators and ensuring measurement of the effects of IDA-supported interventions on higher-order country objectives.

Source: IEG analysis of World Bank 2005a.

---

with the government's own strategy and focused on well-specified objectives (box 2.2). Progress was monitored against benchmarks and yielded good results in the reduction of both income and non-income poverty. In China, the Bank recognized that its lending accounts for only a small share of resource flow and relied mostly on policy dialogue through analytical work and the demonstration effect of successful projects to leverage policy outcomes (IEG 2005f). In Brazil, the Bank's strategy in the 1990s and early 2000s became more selective. The program's main component focused on the poor Northeast and on activities expected to address directly the roots of poverty, particularly lending in support of human development and to improve access of the poor to basic infrastructure (IEG 2004d).

Unsuccessful assistance strategies are frequently overly ambitious[5]

Over-ambition is a widespread characteristic of Bank assistance programs. About half of all the Country Assistance Strategies reviewed and evaluated by IEG over the past four fiscal years were assessed as having been too ambitious. Ninety percent of assistance programs in the subsampled countries where poverty was not reduced and where the Bank's assistance failed to deliver the expected results were overly ambitious and not sufficiently tailored to country conditions.

Overly ambitious strategies led to programs that either were not sufficiently selective or established unrealistic expectations for reform programs.

There are two main ways in which Country Assistance Strategies have been overly ambitious. They have either lacked selectivity or they have centered on Bank support for reform programs that were not commensurate with institutional capacity and the political situation in the country. Forty-eight percent of the strategies IEG assessed as overly ambitious fell in the former group and 36 percent fell in the latter, with the remainder suffering from a combination of the two.

Country Assistance Evaluations suggest that several factors can help determine ex-ante whether an assistance strategy is realistic or not. These include past record with reform implementation and realization of Bank assistance programs (including dropped operations in previous assistance programs and implementation delays), judicious analysis of the political economy and implementation capacity in a country, and clear identification of country risks.

Country Assistance Strategies that lacked selectivity led the Bank to spread its resources too thinly across too many sectors, which diluted its effectiveness. This was the case, for example, in Honduras and Malawi, where the Bank's program covered more areas and institutions than could be handled effectively by either the Bank or the country (IEG 2006f, 2006i).

The need to strategically focus Bank assistance on a selected number of important areas is particularly strong in smaller countries and in fragile states. In Cambodia and São Tomé and

Principe, for example, IEG analysis found that the Bank's lending program stretched its resources too thinly across too many sectors, which prevented it from effectively engaging in policy dialogue and supervision.[6]

Overly ambitious strategies have also led to unrealistic expectations for reform programs supported by policy-based lending. In Malawi, for example, the Bank proceeded with policy-based lending for reform programs that were not adequately scaled to country conditions and achieved few sustainable results (IEG 2006i).

The Bank sometimes also proceeded with such lending under external pressure to help prevent default. Its financing then perpetuated unsustainable fiscal situations, without addressing the underlying causes. In Pakistan, two policy-based loans had little sustainable impact on structural reforms, despite the large amounts of funding advanced to avoid default. But a policy-based operation achieved satisfactory results in subsequent years, when it was adequately tailored to local conditions and supported a government-owned reform program (IEG 2006j). In Zambia, external pressure for balance of payment support weakened the design and supervision of successive policy-based operations and delayed privatization of mines and necessary structural reforms (IEG 2002c). In Bolivia, the prolonged high level of aid prevented adherence to hard budgetary constraints and, when a crisis arose, the Bank and other donors were compelled to provide further assistance at a time when its likely effectiveness was most questionable (IEG 2005c). The Bank should be cautious about providing emergency liquidity to avoid default in the absence of a strong reform program.

Analytical work with country participation helps tailor assistance strategies to local conditions

A realistic Country Assistance Strategy requires an accurate assessment of the country's political economy and of the main constraints to poverty-reducing growth. Assistance strategies built on analytical work done in collaboration with local specialists have tended to be more realistic and

resulted in better outcomes. Collaborative work also helps enhance local capacity and build ownership of Bank-supported programs.

Assistance strategies that are not selective spread the Bank's resources too thinly and dilute its effectiveness.

In Brazil, for example, the Bank's strategy was underpinned by high-quality analytical work on poverty and growth, done with substantial participation by top Brazilian researchers (IEG 2004d). In Armenia, the most successful periods of the Bank's assistance were those underpinned by strong analytical work on growth and poverty (box 2.3). A hiatus in analytical work prevented recognition of important constraints to growth and the strategy failed to recognize the need to push the agenda in new directions (IEG 2004a). In Turkey, a broad program of analytical work, often done with substantial participation of Turkish experts, helped build consensus for overdue reforms that proved essential to revitalizing Turkey's economy (IEG 2005n).

Assistance strategies built on analytical work done with local participation have tended to be more realistic and resulted in better outcomes.

Achieving poverty-reducing growth— challenges for Bank assistance

Designing assistance strategies that are well grounded in country analysis, set out realistic expectations, and can contribute to achieving poverty-reducing growth poses a host of challenges. Recent IEG evaluations provide evidence on some of them, including the need to:

- Deepen country analysis to understand what factors in a given country can lead to a pattern of growth that efficiently translates into poverty reduction.
- Find more effective ways to reduce rural poverty.
- Increase attention to the distributional effects of growth-enhancing reforms.
- Find more effective ways to reduce poverty in low-income countries under stress and fragile states (LICUS).

Box 2.3: Analytical Work on the Constraints to Poverty-Reducing Growth Helped Reshape Bank Assistance to Armenia

The study "Growth Challenges and Government Policies in Armenia" demonstrated how poverty-focused analytical work can help shape Bank assistance in support of poverty-reducing growth. It analyzed why the steady rise in Armenia's real GDP during the second half of the 1990s had not led to significant improvements in poverty and employment creation. It found that improvements in wage levels had disproportionately benefited labor in a few sectors that employed a small proportion of total labor. It showed that a poor business climate and weak private sector capabilities hindered the establishment or expansion of private firms. It recommended policies and actions designed to accelerate enterprise restructuring, attract investment, and encourage the creation of new businesses in the medium term. Largely as a result of this analysis, the Bank's assistance was redirected to support government efforts to improve the overall business climate, rather than pursuing privatization in isolation.

Source: IEG 2004a.

They also illustrate the circumstances in which the Bank can effectively help cushion the impact of a crisis.

Paying attention to the pattern of growth

The ability of the poor to participate in growth depends on how much growth is driven by productivity increases in sectors where a large number of the poor work, how much growth translates into job creation, and how well the poor are equipped to take advantage of such job growth. Growth in more labor-intensive sectors and in sectors where large numbers of the poor work, such as agriculture and manufacturing, has been found to lead to more poverty reduction than growth in less labor-intensive sectors, such as mining or utilities (Christiaensen, Demery, and Kühl 2006; Loayza and Raddatz 2005; Ravallion and Chen 2004).

This does not mean that countries should not invest in sectors with low labor intensity, but it does suggest that they should pursue a strategy that balances growth in those sectors with growth in sectors that have the potential to absorb a higher share of labor. Strategies for poverty reduction thus need to consider where the poor live, how they earn their income, and what constrains growth in those areas. They also need to consider the constraints to intersectoral

Strategies for poverty reduction need to consider where the poor live and how they earn their income.

mobility of the poor, such as low skills or lack of access to capital, infrastructure, or market outlets. Identifying such constraints and devising the proper response is an involved task and will require country-level research and analysis, which the Bank and other donors can support.

In the subsample of countries that experienced positive growth without poverty reduction, growth was concentrated in subsectors with low labor intensity and where few of the poor could earn their incomes. The Bank's assistance often contributed to bringing these countries back to a growth path through improved economic management, but it was less successful in bringing about job-creating growth. In Georgia, for example, the oil transport sector was a major driver of growth, but it created little employment.[7] The Bank Group's assistance was successful in helping to reestablish macroeconomic stability and contributed to growth in the oil transport sector through related infrastructure investments, but it was less successful in helping to remove obstacles to more broad-based growth. In Madagascar, the Bank's assistance strategy sought to put the country back on a sustained growth path by putting the overextended public sector on firmer ground and by establishing the conditions necessary for private sector growth. It focused on sectors with high growth potential that would allow for relatively quick payoffs, but their impact on poverty was limited. The strategy succeeded in bringing the country back to a growth path, but the growth was concentrated in a few export-oriented sectors that created only limited and cyclical urban employment. It thus made few inroads into poverty, although preliminary data suggest that recent reforms in the rural sector may have led to poverty reduction over the past two years (IEG 2006h).

Many resource-rich countries, among them Madagascar, Nigeria, and Zambia, have performed well below their potential over the past decade. Underperformance in resource-rich countries has been linked to unsound revenue management and poor governance. While Country Assistance Strategies suggest that the Bank is aware of the main reasons for underperformance in such countries, formulating a viable approach to address them remains a challenge (IEG-World Bank, -IFC, and -MIGA 2005). The Bank is preparing guidelines for staff on the challenges to consider when developing Country Assistance Strategies for resource-rich countries.

Finding effective ways to reduce rural poverty remains a challenge

Poverty reduction was faster in urban than in rural areas in the majority of the relevant subsample countries. The rural poor continue to outnumber the urban poor in all subsample countries except Brazil and Uruguay, which have a high urbanization rate[8] (appendix D). The incidence of poverty remains higher in rural areas than in urban areas in most of the subsample countries (figure 2.8).

Country Assistance Evaluations show that the Bank has found it challenging to help countries formulate and implement strategies that effectively reduce rural poverty. Of the full sample of 48 Country Assistance Strategy reviews completed by IEG over the past four fiscal years, about half concluded that the Bank's assistance in rural areas did not lead to satisfactory results and/or that rural poverty reduction required increased attention.

Performance was particularly weak in Africa. In some countries the strategy supported by the Bank has been based on the premise that the engine of growth needs to be jump-started in urban areas. But insufficient attention has often been paid to strengthening urban-rural linkages and to implementing strategies that also help improve farm and off-farm productivity in rural areas. In Senegal, the poverty focus of Bank lending came late, and with a strong bias in favor of urban areas (IEG 2006q). In Malawi, where poverty has remained unchanged over the past decade, the Bank attempted to address rural development issues through adjustment lending and largely failed to help the government develop policies to address low agricultural productivity and food security (IEG 2006i). In Pakistan, the Bank's rural assistance program lacked vision and insufficiently addressed rural poverty (IEG 2006j).

Even in transition economies and some middle-income countries in Latin America, IEG Country Assistance Evaluations conclude that the Bank should focus more on rural poverty. In Armenia, as in a number of other countries of the former Soviet Union, increased focus on rural poverty reduction was highlighted as a priority for future Bank involvement because few inroads have been made into rural poverty, despite strong growth (IEG 2004a). In Honduras, the Bank's economic and sector work needs to intensify research on new economic opportunities for the poor, particularly in the agricultural sector, and future Bank support needs to include a focus on improving agricultural growth (IEG 2006f). Even in Brazil, where the majority of the poor live in urban areas, the Bank and governments need to

Many resource-rich countries have performed below their potential.

Half of IEG's country assistance reviews concluded that assistance in rural areas either did not yield satisfactory results or that rural poverty reduction required more attention.

Strengthening urban-rural linkages and increasing rural productivity require more attention.

Figure 2.8: Poverty Remains More Widespread in Rural than in Urban Areas in Most of the Sampled Countries

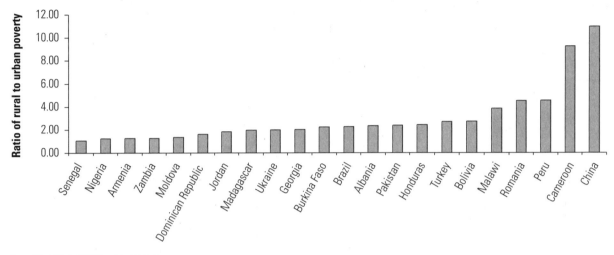

Source: World Bank, DECRG poverty database.

find ways to increase agricultural productivity outside the large commercial agricultural sector to help curb rural poverty (IEG 2004d).

In countries where rural poverty remains pervasive, future Bank assistance will need to focus more on working with governments to identify ways to establish stronger urban-rural linkages and increase intersectoral mobility, as well as strategies that improve productivity in the rural sector.

Some reforms entail undesirable distributional effects[9]

Not all pro-growth policies have a positive or neutral impact on income distribution.[10] The empirical literature suggests that sound macroeconomic policies, access to infrastructure, and educational attainment tend to improve income distribution. But the literature also finds that the impact of financial sector liberalization, trade reform, and the size of government on income distribution varies, depending on such factors as existing distortions and the extent of complimentary reforms undertaken (see World Bank 2006h for a summary of the literature).

> *Not all pro-growth policies have a positive or neutral impact on income distribution.*

For example, some have found that financial sector liberalization has a positive effect on income distribution by creating enhanced conditions for entrepreneurial investments that generate employment (see, for example, Chhibber and Nayyar 2006). Financial sector liberalization can also positively affect income distribution if the lower-income groups gain access to credit. Others have found that such liberalization can result in increasing inequality during the early stages of financial sector development if financial sector institutions are geographically concentrated or if gaining access to credit involves large setup costs for low-income groups, so that they initially remain outside the formal credit markets. But they have also found that as the financial sector develops further and a larger share of the population gains access to credit over time, income distribution eventually improves (see World Bank 2006h).

IEG's evaluation of Bank assistance for trade policy reform found that the reforms had mixed effects on employment and poverty, depending on the extent of both complementary reforms and diversification in the economy. At times, short-term adjustments led to worsening income distribution, while the longer-term effects on poverty were positive because they enhanced growth (IEG 2006c).

The Bank has not always paid sufficient attention to the distributional effects of growth-enhancing reforms. As a result, the effects of the pro-growth reforms it supported were not always cushioned by safety net interventions. In trade reform, for example, the Bank often failed to conduct sufficient analysis to inform its policy advice and lending about the employment and poverty effects of reforms. Consequently, trade-related projects did not adequately attend to these effects (IEG 2006c). Similarly, in many transition economies, price and exchange rate liberalizations were not accompanied by the necessary offsetting measures to protect food security and provide social safety nets (IEG 2004e). In its support for reforms of pension systems, the Bank's assistance focused primarily on improving the fiscal sustainability of pension systems, but it often failed to sufficiently address the pension system's primary goal of reducing poverty and providing adequate old-age income within fiscal constraints (IEG 2006k). Efforts to promote private sector participation in the power sector were found to require more focus on how the poor can be assured of access to energy (IEG-World Bank, -IFC, and -MIGA 2003).

Given the demonstrated importance of distributional changes to poverty reduction, an increased focus on the distributional impact of Bank-supported reforms at the country level is needed. The Bank has recently prepared guidelines for staff on analyzing the distributional impact of reforms.

Many Organisation for Economic Co-operation and Development (OECD) countries use taxes and transfers to smooth income inequality. Transfers from the rich to the poor and from the working to the nonworking have been found to lower the Gini inequality measure by up to 18 percentage points in some OECD countries.[11] Income transfers can help the poor obtain education and health services and protect against risks of losing income—for example, by

allowing children to stay in school or credit-constrained poor people to take up productive opportunities. On this premise, several middle-income countries have initiated poverty-targeted income transfers that are conditional on beneficiaries investing in education, and often on participating in maternal and child health programs.

The distributional effects of growth-enhancing reforms have not always received sufficient attention.

The Bank has widely supported conditional cash transfer programs in Latin America, and more recently in such countries as Bangladesh, Pakistan, and Turkey.[12] Evaluations indicate that the transfers can be an effective way to invest in human capital among poor households, while also reducing poverty, and can even lead recipients to invest part of the transfer in income generation (box 2.4).

Conditional cash transfers can help reduce poverty and invest in human capital formation of the poor.

To attain the intended objectives, these operations must be supported by improvements in the supply and quality of health and education services when the existing capacity is not sufficient to respond to the increased demand by program beneficiaries. Because these programs are costly, they need to be carefully targeted. It may also be necessary to make trade-offs between coverage and size of transfers.

The long-term impact of these programs remains to be assessed. The sustainability of behavioral changes and the effectiveness of conditional cash transfers as a mechanism to address chronic—as distinct from transient—poverty still need further evaluation. Also unclear is the extent to which such programs could be effective in countries with weaker institutional capacity, including lower-income countries.

Many OECD countries use taxes and transfers to smooth income inequality.

Box 2.4: Conditional Cash Transfers Help Latin American Families Increase Human Capital Formation

Conditional cash transfer programs in many Latin American countries provide cash assistance to poor families in exchange for beneficiary compliance with human development actions, such as school attendance or participation in health programs. These programs have demonstrated positive impacts on education, health, and poverty reduction.

School Attendance—*Mexico* increased secondary enrollment for girls by 14 percent and boys by 8 percent. *Brazil* achieved a net 3-percentage-point increase in school attendance within the target group. In *Nicaragua*, school enrollment for targeted children increased by 18 percent and attendance by 30 percent. In *Columbia*, school attendance for children between 12 and 17 increased by 10 percentage points in rural areas. In *Ecuador*, primary school enrollment increased by 10 percentage points.

Reduction in Child Labor—In *Nicaragua*, with increased enrollment, the percentage of working children between ages 7 and 13 declined by 5 percentage points. In *Mexico*, the probability of children of ages 8–17 working decreased by 10–14 percent.

Health—*Mexico's* program increased child growth by 16 percent among participating children ages 1–3 years. It also reduced child illness by 12 percent, while participating adults were 17 percent less incapacitated by illness. *Colombia's* program increased the height of participating children from 0–2 years by .76 centimeters, weight by .3–.5 kilograms for children 2–4 years old, and reduced the occurrence of diarrhea from 32.6 percent to 22 percent for rural children under 24 months of age. *Nicaragua* decreased the number of stunted children by 5.5 percentage points and of child illness by 7 to 12 percentage points, and increased immunization rates among beneficiaries by 30 percentage points.

Poverty Reduction—In *Mexico*, there was a 10 percent reduction in poverty and a 45 percent reduction in severe poverty among the target population. In *Argentina*, an extra 10 percent of the participants would have fallen below the food poverty line without the program in 2003. *Colombia's* program helped reduce extreme poverty by 6 percent in one year.

Sources: Cardoso and Souza 2004; Ferreira, Leite, and Litchfield 2006; Gertler 2004; Maluccio and Flores 2004; Attanasio and others 2005; Skoufias 2005; Skoufias, Benjamin, and De La Vega 2001.

More effective ways need to be found to reduce poverty in fragile states

Low-income countries under stress (LICUS), also known as fragile states, are home to almost 500 million people, roughly half of whom live on less than a dollar a day. These countries face poor governance, conflict or post-conflict transitions, and a multiplicity of problems that make the achievement of development results particularly challenging.

Awareness of the need to provide development assistance differently in these countries has risen in recent years. The Bank has improved its operational readiness to engage with fragile states, and substantial progress has been made on donor coordination at the international policy level. Significant challenges remain, however. The Bank has generally been effective in contributing to macroeconomic stability and

The Bank has effectively contributed to macroeconomic stability and the delivery of physical infrastructure in post-conflict countries.

delivering physical infrastructure in the immediate post-conflict phase, but the Bank's effectiveness needs to be improved following this phase, when structural change is needed.

The Bank still has to sufficiently internalize political understanding in its LICUS country strategies. For example, the Interim Strategy for Papua New Guinea contained a good discussion of the political system and recognized problems such as clan loyalties, political patronage, corruption, and lack of capacity, yet it treated these problems as technical in nature and did not directly use this knowledge to underpin the overall approach.

Strong donor coordination at the international policy level still needs to be carried over to the country level. In adopting state building as one of its two main objectives, the Bank has made an area of traditional weakness (capacity development and governance) a part of its central focus in LICUS, but it still needs to demonstrate how past weaknesses will be avoided and better capacity development and governance outcomes ensured (IEG 2006r).[13]

Bank support can help cushion the impact of a crisis

The Bank's assistance has yielded satisfactory outcomes, even in some countries where poverty stagnated or increased. This was, for example, accomplished when Bank assistance helped the government weather a crisis and then supported the implementation of structural reforms to bring the economy back onto a growth path.

In Uruguay the Bank quickly changed its assistance strategy to support the government's adjustment program following the 2002 financial crisis, which helped to cushion the impact of the crisis. The Bank's program successfully supported fiscal consolidation, financial sector reforms, and measures to enhance the efficiency of poverty reduction programs. At the same time, it supported social and infrastructure investments that helped improve access of low-income groups to these services.[14] In Turkey, a portfolio cleanup and a concerted effort by the Bank to sharpen the strategic focus of its assistance program produced significant improvements in the Bank's dialogue with the authorities and allowed the Bank to provide timely policy and financial support in response to the 2001 financial crisis (IEG 2005n).

To swiftly respond to a crisis, the Bank needs strong knowledge of the economy based on prior analytical work. In Turkey, development of the knowledge base in the years before the crisis allowed the Bank to respond quickly when the Turkish authorities recognized the need for decisive action on structural reforms following the financial crises of 1999 and 2001 (IEG 2005n). Similarly, in India and Morocco, in-depth knowledge of the economy acquired through economic and sector analysis positioned the Bank to advise and support governments on the sequencing of macroeconomic, trade, and structural reforms following crises (IEG 2006c).

Where the Bank's support to crisis-ridden countries had successful results, it supported a reform program developed and owned by the government, often with elements based on prior analytical work carried out with the Bank. In contrast, where the Bank's assistance to crisis countries did not yield satisfactory results, the Bank, often under external pressure to provide liquidity, proceeded with policy-based lending without government commitment to fiscal adjustment and structural reforms.

But it needs to find better ways to help build capacity and strengthen governance in LICUS.

When the Bank has successfully assisted a crisis-ridden country, it has supported a reform program developed and owned by the government, often underpinned by prior analytical work.

Chapter 3: Evaluation Highlights

- The share of projects with satisfactory outcomes has increased, but even satisfactory project outcomes do not guarantee sector-level results.
- Achieving results in one sector often requires removing constraints in other sectors, which makes the use of a clear results chain essential.
- Combining longer-term objectives with interventions that yield visible short-term results helps achieve sector impact.
- If pressures to show results quickly are not properly managed, the quality of results can be compromised.

Achieving Meaningful Results at the Sector Level

The World Bank's contribution to poverty reduction is achieved through the impact of interventions in various sectors and the overall impact of these interventions on a country's economic and sector-specific performance. This chapter will focus on the factors that enable Bank projects to contribute to sector-level results, particularly in sectors that deliver services to the poor. The chapter draws on the findings of IEG sector and thematic evaluations, Project Performance Assessments, and Country Assistance Evaluations completed over the past four fiscal years.

How Have the Bank's Projects Performed?

The overall performance of the Bank's portfolio has improved over the past five years. The outcomes of over three-quarters of Bank operations were rated moderately satisfactory or better by IEG in fiscal 2001–05, and project outcomes improved in 8 of 14 sectors (figure 3.1).[1] The share of projects with outcomes rated moderately satisfactory or better ranged from lows of 62 percent and 66 percent in private sector development and health, respectively, to above 80 percent in education, transport, and global communications and information technology.

Improvements are also observed in institutional development. Over half of all projects have been evaluated as having achieved a substantial institutional development impact over the past five fiscal years, up from less than 40 percent during the preceding five-year period (appendix A).[2]

The policy environment affects project outcomes

The quality of a country's policies and institutions in a sector affects the outcomes of projects in that sector. The share of projects with satisfactory outcomes is higher in countries with good sector policies, but the correlation of sector policy quality and project outcome varies widely across sectors. It is highest for economic policy, public sector governance, and the financial sector, where most Bank projects are designed to strengthen the relevant policies. The correlation is weakest in health, private sector development, and environment. In these sectors, projects perform

Project outcomes are correlated with the quality of a country's sector policies.

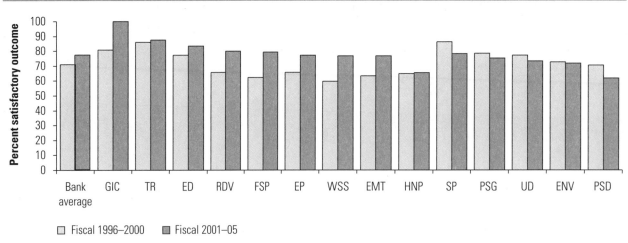

Figure 3.1: Project Outcomes Improved in over Half of All Sectors

☐ Fiscal 1996–2000   ■ Fiscal 2001–05

Source: World Bank database.

Note: Satisfactory project outcomes are all projects rated as moderately satisfactory, satisfactory, or highly satisfactory by IEG. GIC = global information & communications technology; TR = transportation; ED = education; RDV = rural development; FSP = financial sector policy; EP = economic policy; WSS = water supply and sanitation; EMT = energy and mining; HNP = health, nutrition, and population; SP = social protection; PSG = public sector and governance; UD = urban development; ENV = environment; PSD = private sector development.

only slightly better in a good policy environment than they do in a weak one (figure 3.2).

Regression analysis also shows that the likelihood of a project achieving a satisfactory outcome is strongly influenced by the quality of overall economic management in the country and the governance environment, particularly the rule of law. It shows that once income level, economic management, and rule of law are controlled for, there are no regional differences in project success rates (appendix C).

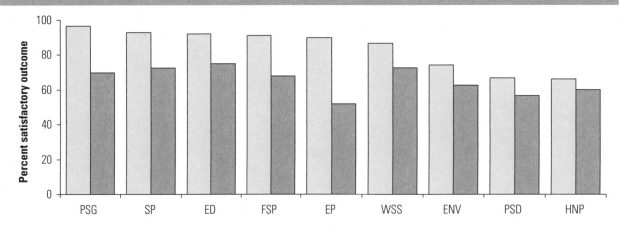

Figure 3.2: Project Outcomes Are Better in Countries with Strong Sector Policies

☐ Good sector policy: sectoral CPIA >3.5   ■ Weak sector policy: sectoral CPIA <=3.5

Source: World Bank database.

Note: Sectors for which no sector-specific CPIA is available are excluded. This accounts for the smaller number of sectors in figure 3.2 compared with figure 3.1. PSG = public sector and governance; SP = social protection; ED = education; FSP = financial sector policy; EP= economic policy; WSS = water supply and sanitation; ENV = environment; PSD = private sector development; HNP = health, nutrition, and population.

How Much Impact Do Projects Have on the Sector?

The Bank intends to achieve more than to simply finance individual projects that meet their immediate objectives. It also aims to help countries strengthen their sectoral policies and institutions to permanently improve services and incomes for the poor. Not every project can be expected to have a sectorwide impact—this often takes a long time and multiple initiatives.

IEG's Country Assistance Evaluations, which typically cover a period of about 10 years, permit a view of the cumulative effect of the Bank's work in a sector. They reveal that it is careful selection and phasing of interventions and the complementarities of lending, analytical work, and policy dialogue that lead to impact on the sector as a whole.

The sector-level impact of Bank assistance, as assessed in the 18 IEG Country Assistance Evaluations completed during fiscal 2004–06, was lowest in public sector, private sector, and rural development. This confirms earlier findings of 25 Country Assistance Evaluations from fiscal 2001–03 (IEG 2005h). Rural and private sector operations

achieved a satisfactory sector impact in only half of the countries; Bank operations in the public sector had a satisfactory sectoral impact in fewer than one-third of the countries assessed. The gap between the high share of satisfactory project outcomes and the lower share of satisfactory sector outcomes is also most marked in these three sectors, illustrating that satisfactory project outcomes alone do not guarantee a substantial country sector impact (figure 3.3 and appendix B).

Satisfactory project outcomes do not ensure country sector impact.

Essential Elements for Achieving Results

IEG Country Assistance Evaluations, Project Performance Assessments, and sector evaluations completed over the past four fiscal years point to six elements that can help lead to stronger sector results:

- The presence of a country-formulated sector strategy
- Realistic objectives
- A clear results chain
- A results-focused information system
- Choice of an appropriate lending instrument

Figure 3.3: Successful Projects Alone Do Not Ensure Sector-Level Impact

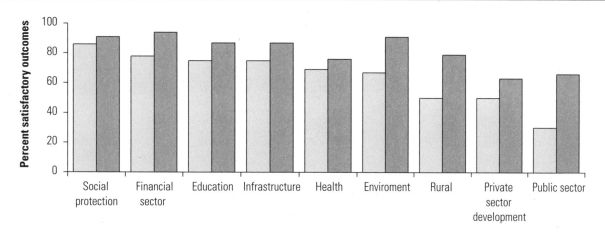

□ Satisfactory sector outcome   ■ Satisfactory project outcome

Sources: World Bank database and Country Assistance Evaluations.

Note: Sector outcomes as assessed by IEG Country Assistance Evaluations (CAEs). The sample includes all CAEs completed in fiscal 2004–06, for a total of 18, but not all CAEs covered all sectors. Projects are those completed in countries where CAEs assessed sector outcomes. "Satisfactory" includes sector and project outcomes rated moderately satisfactory or higher.

- Long-term engagement and striking a balance between long-term and short-term objectives.

Build on a country-formulated sector strategy

Bank interventions have yielded substantially better results when they have supported a country-formulated and broadly owned sector strategy with clear objectives. This is particularly true for interventions that support an overall sectoral reform agenda.

Bank interventions have yielded better results when they have supported a country-formulated sector strategy.

The Bank and other donors can support the formulation of such a sector strategy through analytical work, policy dialogue, and institutional capacity building, but to achieve sustainable results, the strategy needs to be formulated by the country itself. Even well-designed Bank projects can rarely turn around poorly designed sectoral programs, and are thus unlikely to achieve substantial results absent a strong sector strategy. In Albania, for example, the Bank's interventions achieved good results in the power sector, where the government had adopted a clear sectoral reform strategy supported by the Bank through its lending operations. The results of the Bank's assistance in other sectors, where no clear government strategy was in place and where the Bank itself did not have the necessary analytical underpinning, were more modest (IEG 2005a).

Donors can effectively support development and adoption of a sector strategy, provided they recognize that it takes time and a series of interventions. In Cambodia, for example, the Bank's first health sector project helped provide a combination of capacity building and a revised incentive framework at the central and local levels as a catalyst for fundamental changes in the relations between the Ministry of Health and the provinces. As a result, the ministry evolved from a weak bystander to the owner and implementer of national health strategies in collaboration with

Unrealistic targets risk perceived failure, regardless of what might actually be achieved.

international donors (IEG 2004i). Similarly, joint analytical work and support provided under a Bank-financed investment project helped Armenia formulate a comprehensive education sector reform strategy that the Bank helped implement through sector investment and policy lending (IEG 2004a).

Set realistic objectives and targets

An important step in obtaining meaningful sector results is to set realistic targets that are grounded in country analysis, informed by past performance and international experience. Unrealistic targets can generate a perception of failure, regardless of what has actually been achieved. And perceived failure can lead to disillusion and negatively affect future efforts.

In the Bank, as elsewhere, there has been a tendency to adopt unrealistic goals. The Millennium Development Goals (MDGs), for example, are the most widely embraced sectoral targets and have been useful in galvanizing the support of the international community toward achieving defined sector results. But many of these targets set unrealistically high expectations of what a country can achieve by 2015. For example, many countries that started with low primary education school enrollments in 1990 would need to perform as well or better than the historically best performers, such as Korea, to achieve the MDG of universal completion of primary education by 2015 (figure 3.4). Thus, it is not surprising that a considerable number of countries in Sub-Saharan Africa and South Asia that have made substantial progress toward MDG targets are still unlikely to reach those goals, which puts at risk the momentum gained so far.

Unrealistic targets have characterized many Bank-supported projects. Several loans with financial sector components in crisis countries, for example, had ambitious and unrealistic targets driven by an overestimation of the government's commitment to reform, combined with a need to justify large loan amounts. In Indonesia, for example, a series of loans following the 1997 crisis addressed resolution of the banking crisis and

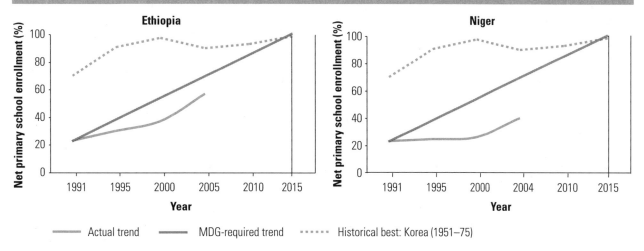

Figure 3.4: Setting Unrealistic Targets Leads to Perceptions of Failure, Even When Substantial Results Are Achieved

Sources: Korea Educational Development Institute 2005, World Bank 2006n.

Note: In the absence of historical data on primary school completion and net enrollments, gross enrollments are shown here for one of the historically best performers, Korea. Reaching a 100 percent primary school completion rate (MDG2) is substantially more challenging than achieving gross enrollment rates of 100 percent or higher. Thus, the primary education MDG would require even stronger performance than the historically best trend shown here.

corporate restructuring, including the resolution and reprivatization of banks and disposal of assets. But by 2003, although the pace of reforms had improved, the government still controlled over 60 percent of the banking system, and the banking sector remained vulnerable to further shocks (IEG 2006g).

Similarly, education projects with designs to improve management performance often set overly ambitious objectives. As a result, only about a quarter of Bank projects reviewed by IEG's recent assessment of assistance for primary education met their targets for improving planning, policy making, and budgeting activities (IEG 2006e). In many cases, project objectives are not grounded in thorough institutional analysis, which can lead to setting unrealistic objectives (box 3.1).

Clear and realistic objectives help achieve results

When objectives are clear and realistic and stakeholders focus on them, they can be achieved. In Bolivia, for example, Bank support in the health sector focused on areas where Bolivia lagged most, infant and maternal mortality. A series of three credits over a decade concentrated on improving the quality and accessibility of essential maternal and child health services, particularly for low-income groups. It helped establish a system of preferred access to health care for maternal and child health issues, supported the expansion of health facilities in rural areas, and established a system that carefully monitored inputs and outcomes. This resulted in dramatic improvements in the utilization of these services and in maternal and child health outcomes (IEG 2005c).

In Uruguay, two Bank-supported education sector projects focused on increasing equity in the education system through improved participation of the most disadvantaged students in preschool education and in full-time schools. The projects' targeted interventions led to substantial improvement in learning outcomes among students from low-income families, which reduced the learning gaps between social groups in the country (IEG 2006e).

Unrealistic targets have characterized many Bank-supported projects.

When objectives are set realistically and stakeholders focus on them, they can be achieved.

Box 3.1: Unrealistic Project Objectives Are Often Grounded in Inadequate Institutional Analysis

Objectives for education sector management often have been overly ambitious and not sufficiently grounded in institutional analysis.

The Primary Education Quality Project in Peru aimed to improve educational management at the Ministry of Education and in the schools. But during preparation, the lack of consensus and political will that eventually kept school autonomy and regional decentralization from being implemented was not properly recognized.

Similarly, the government in Pakistan rushed into large Bank-supported social action projects, each allocating more than $100 million to basic education, without a clear understanding of their complex financial management requirements. A good capacity assessment would have revealed the low technical skills at the provincial and district levels, particularly in financial management, as well as a culture of patronage that frequently led to the misallocation of funds.

Source: IEG 2006e.

Define a clear results chain

Bank sector strategies can help focus on results. Seven sector boards have results frameworks and outcome indicators that provide a starting point for Bank staff as they develop results chains that link country development goals with specific Bank operations. Several other sector boards are developing such frameworks. A major challenge will be adapting these generic frameworks to country circumstances (IEG 2006a). A clear results chain offers three benefits:

- It identifies constraints to achieving objectives and specifies actions necessary to remove them (box 3.2).
- It assigns clear responsibilities.
- It identifies the cross-sectoral interventions necessary to achieve the ultimate outcomes.

The results chain helps identify actions to achieve objectives

The analysis needed to develop a clear results chain is frequently overlooked. In Albania, for instance, the Bank did not pay enough attention to how ambitious goals for governance, health, and education would actually be achieved. Conditions for the Poverty Reduction Support Credit (PRSC) focused mostly on the passage and enactment of laws, which were necessary but not sufficient to achieve the desired objectives in governance. Inadequate attention was given to capacity constraints that hindered effective implementation of these laws. In contrast, in the energy sector the government and the Bank agreed on a specific action plan for reform with monitorable indicators, and satisfactory results were achieved (IEG 2005a). The

---

Box 3.2: Understanding the Results Chain Was Key to Designing Interventions to Improve Girls' School Enrollment in Egypt

In Egypt, gender disparities in primary school enrollment were thought to be cultural in nature, but a series of studies found several other reasons why parents did not send their girls to school: the distance of schools from home, the presence of male teachers, and the quality of education. In 1996, the government launched the Education Enhancement Program, supported by the World Bank and the European Union. The program dealt directly

with those problems by increasing the number of schools in rural areas, improving teacher training, and including gender sensitivity in teacher training programs. This increased parental demand for girls' education and gave a second chance to girls who may have dropped out. As a result of these interventions, the gender gap in primary education has been substantially narrowed over the past five years.

Source: World Bank 2005h.

Bangladesh Integrated Nutrition Project had disappointing outcomes for birth weight, even though participation was high. In this case, the results chain missed two important links: it neglected the role of men and mothers-in-law in nutritional choices, and it focused on pregnancy weight gain rather than pre-pregnancy nutritional status (IEG 2005k).

The results chain clarifies responsibilities

A clear results chain and appropriate monitoring help assign responsibilities and measure the performance of the different actors. In Bolivia, for example, the government, with Bank assistance, made significant progress on most of its objectives in heath and education, largely through well-designed interventions that established clear authorities and accountabilities for all involved, ranging from the sectoral line ministries, to regional departments, to municipalities and individual providers (IEG 2005c). The District Health Services Pilot and Demonstration Project in Uganda, in contrast, had a weak results chain and unclear objectives. This caused confusion among national stakeholders and compromised national understanding and commitment. Consequently, the project made little progress in improving health outcomes (IEG 2006p).

The results chain helps identify cross-sectoral constraints

Achieving results in one sector often requires identifying and removing constraints in other sectors. Analysis of the results chain can help identify necessary cross-sectoral interventions that are often overlooked. Addressing cross-sectoral constraints does not necessarily require large cross-sectoral operations, but it does require that the main constraints to achieving core objectives be identified and addressed in a synchronized fashion.

In Bangladesh, for example, Bank support for female secondary schooling has contributed to reductions in child mortality, because a child born to a mother with secondary education is around 80 percent less likely to die than one born to a mother with no education. Rural electrification improved health outcomes as well, because it helped raise incomes, improved the quality of health care, and expanded people's access to health information through the media (IEG 2005k). In areas of Morocco where the Bank helped finance rural roads, agricultural activity picked up, enrollment in primary education increased (faster than in control areas), and the quality of education improved. Improved accessibility was an important factor in retaining better-qualified teachers and lowering absenteeism among both teachers and students in the remote areas that benefited from investments in rural roads (Levy and Voyadzis 1996).

A clear results chain and appropriate monitoring help assign responsibilities and measure the performance of different actors.

Lack of attention to complementary inputs, however, has diminished the impact of infrastructure investments under some of the Bank's community-driven development projects. Although infrastructure construction in scattered communities increased access to schools and health centers, it did not always translate into effective service delivery because of the inadequacy of complementary inputs such as teachers, doctors, and medicines (IEG 2005i). Similarly, the effectiveness of the Bank's support for pension reform has at times been affected by the failure to ensure that the necessary macroeconomic, financial, and institutional conditions were in place for such reforms to achieve the aspired objectives (IEG 2006k).

Achieving results in one sector often requires removing constraints in other sectors.

The Bank's matrix management structure does not encourage staff to work across sectoral boundaries or to address cross-sectoral issues. Despite attempts by the Regions to create multisectoral teams to coordinate community-driven development projects,

The Bank's matrix management structure does not encourage staff to work across sectoral boundaries.

for example, only 9 percent of Bank staff surveyed reported being satisfied or very satisfied with coordination across sectors in these interventions (IEG 2005i).

As the Bank and its partners incorporate sector-defined outcome indicators into operations, they face the challenge of obtaining the information needed to track progress and adjust activities.

Bank task managers report that preparing and implementing PRSCs has led to more cross-sectoral interaction among Bank staff, but note that institutional constraints to working across sectors are apparent in interactions around PRSCs (IEG 2004g). Similarly, the linkages between trade reform and social and economic vulnerably have not been addressed sufficiently in much of the Bank's support for trade reform, partly because the complexity of the issue requires a multidisciplinary team that cuts across the Bank's sector and network boundaries[3] (IEG 2006c). Lack of cross-sectoral coordination has also affected the Bank's assistance for pension reform. At times this has led to different Bank teams providing inconsistent policy advice to the same country (IEG 2006k).

Use a results-focused information system

As the Bank and its partners make progress in incorporating sector-defined outcome indicators into operations, they now face the challenge of obtaining the information needed to track progress and adjust activities. Three kinds of obstacles inhibit the use of information to improve results.

Enhancing country capacity to collect and use performance information helps achieve better sector outcomes.

• *Indicators are not available or are inadequately matched with the objectives.* The Bank's 2000 Urban Strategy, for example, aims to "improve the competitiveness" of urban markets for land, labor, credit, and infrastructure and housing inputs. But less than 10 percent of urban projects address compet-

itiveness because city-level data are scarce for several proposed indicators. Moreover, practitioners are unsure of what competitiveness means in this context and how to put it into practice (IEG 2004f). Many Bank-supported HIV/AIDS projects and national AIDS programs have used HIV prevalence (the percent of the population that is HIV-positive) as an indicator of the impact of prevention activities. HIV prevalence can rise or fall, depending on whether more people become infected than die over a given period, so it is not an appropriate indicator to measure success in HIV prevention or treatment[4] (IEG 2005g). Most indicators in community-driven development projects focus on quantity of outputs rather than their quality, which makes it impossible to assess project impact on strengthening local capacity (IEG 2005i).

• *Appropriate data are not collected.* The standard outcome indicators for the water supply and sanitation sector are the numbers of people with access to improved drinking water and improved sanitation. About two-thirds of fiscal 2005 water supply and sanitation projects included these outcome indicators, but only one-third of the projects had a baseline against which to measure outcomes (World Bank data). Despite considerable emphasis on monitoring and evaluation systems in Bank-supported HIV/AIDS programs, projects are frequently launched without baseline data that are critical to program design (IEG 2005g).

• *Data collection instruments are poorly designed.* Even when indicators are properly chosen and data are collected, the resulting information may not allow assessment of the impact of project or program interventions if surveys are improperly designed. Repeated national surveys to assess the impact of donor-supported HIV/AIDS programs in Cambodia, Chad, India, and Uganda, for example, failed to ensure the comparability of questions across surveys, which made it impossible to track changes in behavior over time (IEG 2005g). Where Bank operations have successfully helped establish country capacity to collect and use performance information, that information has contributed to better sector outcomes. In Bolivia, for example, the Bank promoted the idea that there was a need to collect detailed statistics on inputs, outputs, and outcomes at the regional level to judge the performance of regional administrators. Consistent application of this approach under Bank-supported health and education sector operations has contributed to substantial improvement in Bolivia's health and education sector outcomes (IEG 2005c).

Choose the appropriate lending instrument

To enhance the sector impact of its operations, the Bank has gradually shifted emphasis from specific investment projects toward supporting sectorwide initiatives through development policy and programmatic lending. Such sectorwide initiatives have taken three main forms: replacement of sector-specific operations with components in multisector development policy lending operations; combination of multisector development policy lending and sector-specific operations; and dedicated sectorwide operations. These emerging approaches have had varying results.

Multisector operations can dilute sectoral ownership and oversight

Where sector-specific operations were replaced by sector components of multisector operations, the transition has often not been smooth and outcomes have been mixed. In the shift to budgetary support, the need for continued capacity building in the line agency often has not been considered. The institutional reforms that accompany policy adjustments usually take longer than the time allotted in quick-disbursing operations. In Burkina Faso, for example, the transition from project to programmatic support resulted in only limited involvement of the sector line agencies and Bank sector teams in the PRSC-related sector dialogue, as both sides grappled with the shift of attention from project-specific issues to the sector budget as a vehicle for sector dialogue and instrument to achieve results. In the health sector, this led to weak ownership of the health sector program supported under the PRSC by the Ministry of Health.[5] Ultimately, the Bank

decided to supplement the PRSC support for health reforms with a sector-specific operation.

The sectoral impact of multisector operations has often been weaker than that of sector-specific operations, partly because multisector operations allow for less-intensive engagement of Bank sector teams with country line agencies. In the financial sector, for example, the outcome of loans overseen by Bank financial sector departments was substantially better than financial sector components of multisector loans (IEG 2006g). Similarly, pension-specific loans and pension reform components of development policy lending operations led by the social protection and financial sector departments achieved better outcomes than pension components of multisector operations led by economic policy teams (IEG 2006k). In the education sector, multisector operations with education components, such as PRSCs, have helped boost educational enrollments, but they have contributed little to improving educational quality and learning outcomes (IEG 2006e).

The shift from sector-specific operations to sector components of multisector operations has not always been smooth.

Sector-specific operations have tended to have greater sector impact than multisector operations.

A combination of policy-based lending and sector-specific operations can deliver good results in countries where there is strong commitment to sector reforms but limited capacity to implement them. In Armenia and Ghana, for example, the Bank effectively used development policy lending to support reforms in the education sector, while parallel investment projects helped build the systems and capacity to implement the reforms (IEG 2004a, 2006e). The combination of policy-based and technical assistance lending has also yielded better results in financial sectors in low-income countries. The same has not been true for financial sector support to middle-income countries, where the existence of a technical assistance loan in addition to policy-based lending for financial sector reforms may indicate lack of government commitment to carry out the reforms, rather than limited capacity (IEG 2006g).

Sectorwide approaches

To enhance the impact of sector-specific support, the Bank is increasingly participating in a sectorwide approach, or SWAp.[6] While there is not yet a comprehensive evaluation of this experience, an initial review of project outcomes and lessons learned from the first set of completed SWAps suggests that they have generally succeeded in strengthening country ownership for reforms and in enhancing capacity to set policies and strategic direction.[7]

A better balance between support for strategy and policy formulation and for building technical and implementation capacity is needed in sectorwide approaches.

They have been less successful in building capacity to manage the sector for results and to improve service delivery. There are three main reasons for this:

- First, the focus and interaction with government has largely been limited to the policy level, with the Bank and other donors paying less attention to technical issues and details of implementation.
- Second, because of their sectorwide focus, many of the operations have been too complex in relation to local implementation capacity.
- Third, the effort to harmonize approaches and systems has required too much attention to processes in relation to actual program implementation.

Some Bank clients in Africa have expressed concern that a focus on strategic issues deprives local sectoral staff of capacity development that traditionally has been provided formally through the implementation of investment projects, and informally through Bank supervision (IEG 2005e). The

The long time often required to achieve intended results underlines the importance of continuity of engagement in a sector.

Bank and other donors need to strike a better balance between providing support for strategy and policy formulation and for building technical and implementation capacity.

Engage for the long term

Many of the intended results of even well-executed sector operations require more time than a single project cycle. In education, for example, international evidence shows that student performance often drops in the first five years after initiation of a sector reform, before the benefits of even a well-designed and well-implemented program take hold and learning outcomes improve (IEG 2006e). Therefore, expectations of what can be achieved in the time span of a single Bank operation must be managed, and feasible intermediate objectives defined for each operation.

The long time often required to achieve intended results underlines the importance of continuity of engagement in a sector. IEG's evaluation found, for example, that continued Bank support to the health sector in Bangladesh over three decades has contributed to remarkable improvements in the country's maternal and child health outcomes, while such results were not clearly discernable after the first decade of assistance (IEG 2005k). An evaluation of the Bank's urban portfolio found that projects that followed on and integrated the lessons learned from previous projects achieved better results than other projects, which underlines the benefits of continuity of Bank engagement (IEG 2004f).

Balancing short-term and long-term objectives improves results

Although achieving high-impact results takes time, pressure to show results quickly is inevitable. Such pressures, if not managed well, can compromise the quality of results. In many low-income countries, the objective of achieving universal completion of primary education by 2015 has led to massive efforts to expand coverage of the education system. While getting more children to attend school is an important achievement, such rapid expansion has often been at the expense of attention to learning outcomes. For example, in Uganda, enrollment expansion was dramatic, but was not accompanied by sufficient expansion of physical facilities and books, and learning outcomes plummeted. By 2005, there were an average of 94 students per classroom and 3 students were sharing a single textbook (IEG 2006e).

Few Bank-supported education projects have focused sufficiently on striking a balance between rapid expansion of coverage and building the systems and institutional capacity to ensure that learning outcomes are not negatively affected by rapid expansion. Only one-third of primary education operations assessed by IEG explicitly aimed to improve learning outcomes. Yet the experience of Ghana, India, and Uruguay shows that it is possible to expand access and improve student learning simultaneously, but only with careful strategic planning, beginning with planning to improve learning outcomes and ensuring political commitment to that goal.

The approach taken to implement policies to achieve these objectives differed across the three countries, as did Bank support, highlighting the importance of tailoring support to country conditions. While Bank support focused primarily on providing learning inputs in Ghana, in India it consisted of a mixture of learning inputs and support of pedagogical renewal, while in Uruguay it targeted interventions, such as better access of disadvantaged children to preschool and extra instructional time to improve learning outcomes (IEG 2006e).

The pressure to show results quickly can be particularly strong in post-conflict situations. In Uganda, the Bank-supported District Health Services Pilot and Demonstration Project was designed as a pilot to demonstrate the feasibility of delivering an essential health services package. But under pressure to quickly expand support during the post-conflict period, project activities were expanded country-wide without the benefit of evaluating each phase and adjusting sector reforms based on experience. As a result, the project failed to achieve its overarching objectives of reducing disparities in access and improving maternal and child health outcomes (IEG 2006p). In Timor-Leste, the breakdown of government institutions, poor governance, widespread suffering, and massive displacement of the population put pressure on the international community to respond speedily. The Bank's three Community Empowerment Projects (CEP-I, II, and III) quickly transferred resources to communities and delivered massive amounts of infrastructure. But speed came at the cost of the other project objectives, particularly community empowerment and the development of local institutions (IEG 2006o).

Where Bank support combined longer-term objectives with interventions that yielded visible short-term benefits, it has achieved good results. In Cambodia, for example, the Bank successfully took a longer-term approach from the outset of its support to the country's health sector, investing heavily in government capacity and health infrastructure while supporting programs to control communicable diseases that yielded visible results over a shorter period (IEG 2004i). Similarly, in Ghana, the Bank's support to the education sector mixed support for policy reforms with funding for school infrastructure and teaching materials over a 15-year period. This steady stream of visible physical outputs helped garner the support needed for the reforms necessary to expand coverage and gradually improve learning outcomes (IEG 2004c).

If pressure to show results quickly is not managed well, the quality of results can be compromised.

Where the Bank combined longer-term objectives with interventions that yielded short-term benefits, it achieved good results.

Chapter 4: Evaluation Highlights

- To succeed, technocratic reform programs need strong political support and a focus on enforcement capacity.
- Process reforms need to be supported by efforts to raise the demand for accountability and increased transparency.
- Bank operations have helped foster accountability by bringing transparency to a variety of public management processes.
- Stronger community participation can raise the demand for accountability of public sector institutions.

Strengthening Public Sector Accountability

Achieving and sustaining growth and poverty reduction require public institutions that perform well and are accountable to stakeholders for the results achieved. This chapter reviews how the Bank has worked with governments to strengthen the effectiveness and accountability of public sector institutions. It draws on emerging lessons from IEG Country Assistance Strategy reviews carried out over the past four fiscal years, as well as recent thematic evaluations on community development, extractive industries, and fiduciary assessments.

The Bank's Country Assistance Strategies put substantial emphasis on strengthening public sector institutions. For instance, among 48 countries covered in IEG's recent Country Assistance reviews, 42 emphasized strengthening public sector performance or reducing corruption, although an active Bank lending program in this area materialized in only 35 of these countries. Bank-wide, about one-quarter of all lending operations and 23 percent of commitments have targeted public sector governance and the rule of law over the past five fiscal years. Nearly half of the prior actions for development policy operations are related to governance, particularly public financial management (World Bank 2006m).

The Bank's work to improve the effectiveness and accountability of public sector institutions has focused on initiatives that address institutional aspects of public sector governance, such as civil service and administrative reforms, improved public financial management, tax and customs reforms, and creating an enabling environment for the private sector. More recently, efforts have also been stepped up to strengthen complementary aspects of governance, such as public participation, information disclosure, and reduction of corruption.

Strengthening Accountability with Administrative Reforms

The bulk of the Bank's support has focused on strengthening public sector accountability through reform programs in public administration and public financial management. In almost one-third of the 48 Country Assistance

The Bank has focused on reforms in public administration and public financial management to strengthen public sector accountability.

Strategies reviewed, the Bank-supported reforms were aimed at making the public service more professional, and almost three-quarters contained efforts to improve public financial management, including procurement.

These efforts have helped strengthen the quality of government processes in some countries (figure 4.1). But there is little evidence that the process improvements have yet led to improvements in perceived quality of governance. In most countries assessed by IEG where the Bank program included public sector reforms, governance perception indicators have changed little since the mid-1990s (figure 4.2 and appendix E).[1]

This inertia points to the fact that improvements in processes take time to manifest themselves and affect perception. Yet, in at least two countries, Bulgaria and Lithuania, perceived governance indicators have improved. This demonstrates that it is possible to make rapid progress when there is strong country commitment to do so. The Bank can provide governments with the tools to strengthen the

government processes necessary to improve the governance environment, but effective utilization of such tools remains in the hands of country decision makers.

Country Assistance Evaluations point to three factors that have attenuated the effectiveness of the Bank's efforts to strengthen public sector accountability through large-scale administrative reforms:

- Reform initiatives have not been aligned with political realities.
- They have focused on the adoption of legislation and the establishment of institutions, while neglecting the need for enforcement capacity.
- They have not addressed the intersection between the public sector and private sector, where there is most room for abuse.

Technocratic public sector reform programs need political backing

Large-scale technocratic reform programs have yielded better results when they have built on strong country leadership and broad-based politi-

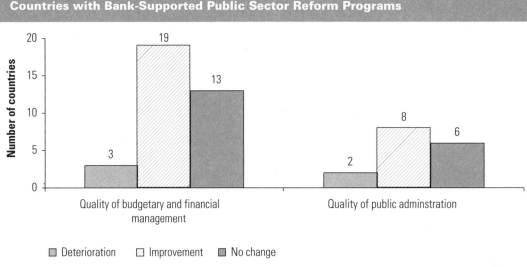

Figure 4.1: Government Process Quality Indicators Improved in About Half of 35 Countries with Bank-Supported Public Sector Reform Programs

□ Deterioration   □ Improvement   ■ No change

Source: World Bank CPIA database.

Note: Quality of government processes indicators used are CPIA for budgetary and financial management and CPIA for quality of public administration from 1999 to 2005. Sample includes all countries where the Bank's assistance program included active support for public sector reform and for which IEG completed a Country Assistance Evaluation or an analysis of a CAS Completion Report in fiscal 2003–06. In 35 of these countries the Bank provided assistance for public financial management, and in 16 it provided assistance for civil service and administrative reform.

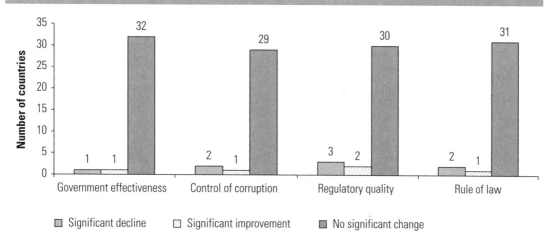

Figure 4.2: But Governance Perception Indicators in 35 Bank Borrowers with Public Sector Reform Programs Did Not Change Significantly

Significant decline ☐ Significant improvement ■ No significant change

Source: Kaufmann, Kraay, and Mastruzzi 2005.

Note: Governance indicators are Kaufmann, Kraay, Mastruzzi Indicators between 1996 and 2004. Classification for deterioration, improvement, and no change is based on a 90 percent confidence interval. Relaxing the confidence interval to 75 percent does not substantially alter the results (appendix E).

Sample includes all countries where the Bank's assistance program included public sector reform and governance activities and for which IEG completed a Country Assistance Evaluation or an analysis of a CAS Completion Report in fiscal 2003–06 and for which governance indicators are available.

Alternative governance indicators, such as those collected by the International Country Risk Group, show a similar picture (see appendix E). The European Bank for Reconstruction and Development–World Bank Business Environment and Enterprise Performance Survey (BEEPS) carried out in countries in Central Asia and Eastern Europe and the former Soviet Union, however, shows improvement in the governance environment in a number of countries in that region over the past three years (see appendix E).

cal support. For instance, public sector reform in Bulgaria, with Bank support, has brought substantial achievements. All new civil service recruitment is conducted through an external process; the pay gap between the public and private sectors has been narrowed, especially at the higher echelons; and functional reviews of ministries are leading to rationalized government structures.[2] While a well-designed reform program supported by a range of donors has played its part, a substantial share of the success of the Bulgarian reforms has been the product of broad-based political support elicited by the prospect of EU accession. Several other transition countries that were offered the possibility of entry to the EU have also improved their governance environments, in contrast with transition countries that did not have such an opportunity (Kaufmann 2006).

When political support has been less forthcoming, the effectiveness of Bank-supported administrative reforms has been undermined. The Public Sector Modernization and Adjustment Credit in Yemen demonstrates the limitations of technocratic changes. The credit aimed to improve the efficiency, effectiveness, and poverty focus of public expenditures. Although all the reforms were at least partly implemented, they have yet to make a difference in civil service performance or public financial management. The civil service ministry, for the first time, has a well-functioning personnel database—a significant achievement—but what it reveals is continued rapid growth in numbers, and thus a failure of establishment controls that casts doubt on the entire reform process. With the civil service nearly twice the size it was when the policy-based operation started, the goal of a modern, well-performing civil service is now further

Large-scale technocratic reform programs have yielded better results when they have enjoyed broad-based political support.

away. The management information system is moving ahead, but it has had little impact on public financial management, which continues to be improper and lax. There has been an improvement in budgeting practices, but a Medium-Term Expenditure Framework to discipline annual budgeting remains to be developed (IEG 2006s).

In Honduras, two public sector reform credits and a PRSC in support of civil service administration and public financial management reforms yielded only limited results, because capacity constraints and political opposition were regularly underestimated. The government's willingness and ability to implement civil service and salary reforms were misjudged at a time when the government team that negotiated a credit in support of these reforms simultaneously undertook steps to increase, rather than reduce, the number and coverage of laws carving out privileged employment and compensation regimes for a large share of public sector employees. As a result, progress toward sustainably reducing the excessively large civil service wage bill remained limited (IEG 2006f).

The Bank has also relied on civil service and public financial management reforms to reduce corruption.

The Bank has had mixed results from its support for public financial management. In about half of the countries for which IEG reviewed the assistance strategy in the past four fiscal years, progress achieved through the Bank's lending in this area has been limited. Particularly in Africa, where public financial management has been a centerpiece of the Bank's support for institutional reforms, it has suffered from limited country ownership of the reform agenda and would benefit from a deeper diagnosis of underlying political and institutional constraints. Efforts to build capacity for institutions have progressed slowly in areas such as procurement and auditing where country ownership has been uncertain. Areas that have received political support, such as tax administration (which promises increased government revenue, at least in the short term), establishment of new institutions with technical mandates, and improvements in basic budgeting, reporting, and accounting systems have made steady progress (IEG 2005d).

In heavily indebted poor counties (HIPCs), substantial efforts have been made to track progress and build capacity for public expenditure management. More than half of the HIPCs have implemented at least 40 percent of the actions in public expenditure management plans they adopted in 2002 (IEG 2006d). The quality of public expenditure management in over half of the HIPCs has improved, as evidenced by a moderate upward trend in HIPC's CPIA scores for budget management (see appendix E).

The Bank has also relied on civil service and public financial management reforms to reduce corruption. Often these have not taken into account the political context. For example, the use of the public service as an employment mechanism is a long-standing political tradition in Bolivia. To counter this, the Bolivian government and the Bank joined together to envisage a frontal attack on corruption called the National Integrity Program. Its implementation relied on civil service reforms and improved public sector financial management, with support from two IDA credits and a half-dozen analytic and advisory efforts. Aimed at developing a stable, professional civil service and establishing standards for procurement, these reforms also would have reduced opportunities for parties to use public sector jobs and contracts as political rewards. The achievements have been modest in relation to objectives and have had a negligible impact on incentives and behaviors in the public sector. The reforms have not been effective because they were fundamentally incompatible with Bolivia's patronage-based governance system (IEG 2005c).

Coalition building and incremental reforms can bring results

When political conditions are not amenable to broad-based public administration reforms, balancing technocratic reforms with coalition building across a broad spectrum of affected interests can help bring results. This may require incremental changes, identifying reform opportunities that are politically acceptable, and creating momentum. In Senegal for example, building political consensus and taking a gradual approach made the difference between successful and unsuccessful regulatory reform in different sectors (box 4.1). Similarly, experience with procurement reforms has shown that they need more than a single champion to succeed. They require active and continuous engagement with key actors such as legislators, external auditors, civil society, and the media to form a critical mass of supporters for the reforms (IEG forthcoming).

New laws and institutions need enforcement capacity

Bank-supported anticorruption efforts have frequently focused on the adoption of legislation and the establishment of institutions and agencies, but frequently failed to ensure that there is adequate enforcement capacity to render these measures effective. In Malawi, where entrenched and worsening corruption afflicts the public service, the Bank has supported the government's Anticorruption Bureau. But there have been few indictments or convictions stemming from cases that the Bureau has investigated, because the cooperation of the Director of Public Prosecutions—a highly politicized office—is needed for a case to proceed. Recently, laws have been enacted to give the Anticorruption Bureau authority to handle its own prosecutions, but the impact of this has yet to be felt (IEG 2006i).

Similarly, in Albania, a specialized small group under the cabinet monitors a broad anticorruption strategy but lacks enforcement power because it has to refer its findings to a prosecutor-general (IEG 2005a). In Madagascar, the government has—with IDA support—put in place a package of reforms including an anticorruption law, agency, and Superior Council; a procurement oversight agency; and mandatory asset declarations for public servants. These measures, while

Balancing technocratic reforms with coalition building helps bring results but requires incremental steps rather than large-scale reforms.

Anticorruption efforts have often focused on new laws and institutions but have given little attention to enforcement capacity.

Box 4.1: Building Coalitions Made for Successful Regulatory Reforms in Senegal

Consensus building has helped reforms in certain sectors in Senegal succeed. The telecommunications sector is now privatized and competitive, despite the opposition of the former state phone monopoly. The reform was successful because it was gradual, involved the opposition political parties, and was based on a transparent bidding process.

In the water sector too, supplies have been improved, at least in urban areas. Water reforms were successful because the Bank and government settled on a public-private lease mechanism that was not the Bank's first choice but was politically acceptable within the Senegalese context.

In electricity, by contrast, privatization has failed. The power company is still fully state-owned, and service is expensive and inefficient. The unsuccessful reform plans were too far-reaching and too dependent on a hoped-for strategic investor.

In urban transport, the goal of fostering private bus companies that would serve the poor has not been achieved. Even though the Bank tried to achieve participatory solutions, the consultative process missed some key leaders who could have helped secure ownership of the reforms.

Source: IEG 2006q.

important, have thus far had a limited impact on the prevalence of corruption, because the independence of the anticorruption agency and Superior Council is in question. Corruption is still perceived to be widespread and endemic (IEG 2006h).

A requirement that public servants declare their financial assets is a standard component of anticorruption programs. Asset declarations have been implemented as part of Bank-supported programs in Albania, Argentina, and Madagascar, for example. To serve their purpose, such declaration requirements must be enforced, verified, and disclosed (box 4.2). In Albania, for one, their effectiveness has been limited by the lack of enforcement mechanisms to track transactions and property ownership (IEG 2005a).

Regulatory and service entities need to be independent of political influence.

The need for enforcement capacity to properly implement legislation aimed at improving transparency and accountability reaches beyond anticorruption efforts. Implementation of prudential regulations and supervision in the banking sector have also suffered from low enforcement capacity. Typ-

The need for stronger enforcement capacity reaches beyond anticorruption efforts.

ically, Bank assistance programs have emphasized legal and regulatory frameworks for the financial sector, but they have underestimated the time and human capacity required to enforce them. Fifteen of 24 countries that had borrowed for legal or regulatory reforms in the financial sector or for strengthening banking supervision had shortcomings in adherence to prudential regulations and lacked enforcement of the prudential framework by the supervisory authority. One of the constraints has been the lack of institutional capacity, including the absence of special enforcement power and legal immunity for supervisors (IEG 2006g, 2004e).

Regulatory and service entities need to be independent of political influence and adequately funded to properly carry out their functions. Independence can be enhanced by techniques such as clear reporting lines, transparency of operations and reports, merit-based personnel rules, and financial self-sufficiency.

Lack of independence has proven an Achilles' heel in otherwise successful programs to upgrade public sector functions. For instance, state water boards in Nigeria are not financially autonomous. They depend on state governments for tariff approvals and many of them are forced to have their staff salaries supplemented by state government budgets. This dependence

---

Box 4.2: Asset Declaration Can Reduce Corruption If It Is Enforced and Disclosed

Requiring public officials to declare their wealth and assets is an article in the United Nations, the African Union, and the Inter-American conventions against corruption. Research using Transparency International's Corruption Perception Indices identified the characteristics that asset declaration laws need to have to work effectively toward reducing corruption:

Constitution: Placing the provision into the country's constitution—intended to signal the high value placed on officials' integrity—does not necessarily translate into reduced corruption.

Ability to prosecute: Perceived corruption is lower in countries whose declaration laws permit the government or anticorruption body to prosecute officials accused of corruption.

Verification: Countries that verify officials' statements have significantly lower corruption than countries that do not.

Disclosure: The laws of some countries require that asset disclosures be placed in the public domain, while others allow only designated government officials to view the declarations. Countries that give public access to officials' asset declaration have significantly lower corruption than those that restrict public access.

Source: Mukherjee and Gokcekus 2006.

makes it impossible for water board managers to improve their financial situation by demanding payment from delinquent but politically connected customers. Indeed, less than half the water the boards supply is actually paid for. As a result, investments in the Kaduna and Katsina Water Boards, financed by the Bank's First Multi-State Water Supply Project, are unlikely to be sustainable (IEG 2006n).

Similarly, in countries such as the Philippines and Uganda, where procurement agencies have a clear mandate, a fair amount of independence, and are adequately resourced, they have successfully helped spur procurement reforms, while in countries where these conditions are not fulfilled, they have proven less successful (IEG forthcoming).

The interface between the private and public sectors is critical for reducing corruption

Opportunities for irregularities occur when the public sector intersects with private firms, particularly in utilities, infrastructure, and extractive industries, where the financial stakes are high. Reforms in these areas have made headway against corruption, even when they have not been part of high-profile anticorruption programs.

Turkey illustrates how reforms aimed at greater cost-effectiveness can also deliver improved integrity. During the 1990s, Turkey's electricity-generation capacity was provided largely through "take-or-pay" contracts between the government and electricity generators. These sole-source contracts not only resulted in inflated prices, but also offered opportunities for government officials to receive illicit payments. By supporting the establishment of an independent regulatory agency, Bank-financed adjustment operations paved the way for direct contracting between sellers and buyers of electric power. This, in turn, has helped to combat corruption at its source (IEG 2005n).

Increased competition, when combined with the right regulatory reforms and supervision, can lead to improved service delivery and accountability of service providers. In Armenia, Bank lending and analytical work was important in advancing energy reforms that included restructuring the sector, tariff increases, reduction of cross-subsidization, and privatization of electricity distribution companies. Between 1993 and 2002, theft of electricity dropped from 30 percent to 10 percent, collections reached 90 percent of billings, and supply interruptions virtually ceased (IEG 2004a).

The progress made in combating corruption through regulatory reforms suggests that sector-specific opportunities to strengthen public sector accountability should be exploited more consistently across the Bank's sectoral operations.

Regulatory reforms have made headway against corruption.

The financial stakes and room for abuse are particularly high in extractive industries. Poor governance and unsound revenue management have been at the core of the overall poor development performance of many resource-abundant countries. An important step in strengthening governance in such countries is to require countrywide and industrywide disclosure of government revenues from extractive industries and related contractual arrangements, such as production-sharing agreements, concessions, and privatization terms. These issues require increased attention by the World Bank Group (IEG-World Bank, -IFC, and -MIGA 2005).

Disclosure of government revenues and contractual arrangements helps strengthen governance in resource-rich countries.

Increasing transparency to foster accountability

Transparency is an essential foundation of good governance and accountability. The benefits of transparency are twofold. First, evidence shows that the access to timely, relevant, and high-quality information reduces the incidence of corruption (Svensson 2005; Recanatini, Prati, and Tabellini 2005). Second, transparent institutions—in the private or public sector—earn the trust and acceptance of the public. This acquired legitimacy strengthens the institutions while encouraging civil participation and promoting accountability. Transparency therefore acts as a regulator of the quality of governance. Lack of transparency in public sector processes offers government officials opportunities for irregular behavior and prevents the citizenry from holding them to account. World Bank operations have sought to bring transparency to a wide variety of public management processes, including public financial management, public procurement, tax and customs administration, the judicial system, and public service provision.

Bank operations have helped bring transparency to a wide variety of public sector management processes.

Measures to enhance *budget transparency* are typically supported by fiscal or macroeconomic policy–based lending operations. In Turkey, extra-budgetary funds that had undermined fiscal discipline were brought into the budget and subjected to parliamentary scrutiny as part of a major post-crisis reform program. Although not primarily aimed at corruption, the dismantling of the extra-budgetary funds was a significant step toward tackling corruption at its source (IEG 2005n). In Albania, the budget preparation process has been debated in Parliament, discussed with nongovernmental organizations (NGOs), and analyzed by the media since 2002 (IEG 2005a).

Public expenditure tracking surveys are used in a growing number of countries to identify leakages of public funds and spark corrective action. In Uganda, for example, an initial survey found that only about 20 percent of conditional grants allocated for schools actually reached them. This prompted a decision to publicize financial allocations at the district and school levels and to improve accountability through public information campaigns. These measures resulted in a substantial improvement in the flow of funds to schools, with subsequent surveys showing that the share of grants reaching the schools had risen from 20 percent to 90 percent (IEG 2004j). These improvements emphasize the role of information in mobilizing "client power" for better expenditure outcomes.

Public procurement is a second important target for increased transparency. In Turkey, a new public tendering system has introduced more transparent bidding procedures, including the publication of winning bids. Such publication is intended to help eliminate the corrupt practice of the government accepting underpriced bids and then, in return for kickbacks, agreeing to cost escalations after contract award (IEG 2005n). Transparency has also enhanced the effectiveness of procurement agencies in the Philippines and in Uganda. In the Philippines, civil society representatives have a mandate to observe the tendering process, and in Uganda procurement audits, final contract awards, and other information are available on public Web sites (IEG forthcoming).

Bank operations have also helped improve transparency of border inspections and *customs administration*. The Trade and Transport Facilitation Program in nine countries of southeastern Europe, which aims to streamline customs procedures and improve efficiency of border crossings, has introduced standard electronic customs forms showing duties payable. This simple measure discourages officials from asking for illicit payments. Some participating countries have added a telephone hotline for truckers to report problems. Recent surveys show that the percentage of businesses reporting customs bribes has decreased in all participating countries but one over the past three years. In Bulgaria, for example, the percentage of businesses reporting customs bribes to be a problem has decreased from 26 percent to 16 percent, according to the Business Environment and Enterprise Performance Survey (World Bank 2006b).

Fostering Local Control to Improve Accountability

The most frequent interaction between state institutions and communities is at the point where services are delivered. Strengthening community voice, participation, and oversight can therefore also elevate the demand for accountability of public institutions and reduce corruption. Mechanisms that promote channels for citizen feedback can raise transparency and accountability, as the experience of Malawi demonstrates. Local initiatives can even handle enforcement where conventional means of redress are ineffective or corrupt (box 4.3).

Development interventions are more likely to generate sustainable results when the local beneficiaries have authority and responsibility for financing and operating them. In the education sector, for example, empowering communities to manage education funds has increased parental involvement in schools and brought improvements in facilities and teacher attendance, although there is little evidence yet that it has improved educational quality (IEG 2006e).

Local control can also ensure that results are sustained and maintained beyond the initial investment period. Nigeria's experience with promoting local participation in the financing and maintenance of water supply systems illustrates the advantages of local control (box 4.4).

Stronger community voice and oversight can raise demand for accountability and reduce corruption.

Community-driven development can strengthen or undermine capacity of local institutions
Bank-financed operations support local and community control, both through direct support to local governments and through community-driven development (CDD) initiatives that give control over planning decisions and investment resources to community groups and local governments. CDD projects span a broad range of sectors and activities and pursue a variety of objectives.

Box 4.3: Using Community Feedback to Enhance Accountability

The ongoing third *Malawi Social Action Fund Project* uses community scorecards to allow citizens to assess the performance of local public services and agencies and thereby foster better quality, efficiency, and accountability. Using participatory techniques, more than 500 communities throughout Malawi have scored local agencies' performance on their management processes and the performance of project outputs such as water points and classroom blocks. At the same time, the agencies also do a self-assessment. The community and the agency then meet to agree on a joint action plan for reform or performance improvement.

The first round of scores was less than satisfactory. Communities complained about lack of transparency. They suggested that local authorities need to allow communities to participate more fully. In order to curb the problem of "ghost workers," they recommended that local project committees verify that the number of people receiving wages equals the number who actually worked.

While not yet independently assessed, the scorecard process appears to be making communities aware of their role in the management of subprojects and local authorities seem to be becoming more responsive to citizen complaints. The project is now working with local authorities and partners to adopt the process as a regular part of local government.

The *Kecamatan Development Project (KDP) in Indonesia* included an innovative strategy to attack Indonesia's deeply ingrained corruption. One part of the strategy provides for systematic procedures for local authorities to follow up instances of corruption reported by villagers, including through a "complaints box." In many such cases, inferior work was rectified, and in a few cases funds were returned or (rarely) officials removed from office. Such sanctions are almost always the result of villager appeals to higher-level officials. Complaints through the police and judicial channels have proved of little use; the police can be bribed and the judicial system is unable to act on complaints against officials. The positive effects of improved community-based enforcement may, however, not have succeeded in reducing the overall level of corruption. A recent impact evaluation found that increasing grassroots participation in monitoring village-level KDP interventions altered the method of possible corruption but had relatively limited effects on the overall level of possible corruption.

Sources: Staff reports and IEG 2006m.

Box 4.4: Local Control of Water Systems Gets Better Results

The Bank's support for water supply in Nigeria initially supported national-level institutions and then shifted to state-level water boards. More recently, a new approach was piloted: demand-driven investments in small towns.

The results have been dramatically different. The national- and state-level entities remain utterly ineffective at providing good quality water and are financially in-

solvent. The 2000 Small Towns Project required the participating towns to contribute financially—through new Water Consumer Associations—to the project investments and to organize sustainable operation and maintenance of the systems they now owned. Twelve of the 16 towns now have functioning water systems, along with good monitoring and evaluation tools to track and report on performance.

Source: IEG 2006n.

CDD projects that establish parallel structures and procedures risk undermining efforts to strengthen local government capacity.

They generally combine delivering local infrastructure or services with building local capacity for decision making and resource management. How effectively these mechanisms contribute to better public services depends on the extent to which they reinforce legitimate institutions.

To ensure efficient delivery of local infrastructure and services, CDD projects have frequently established structures, pro- cedures, and funding mechanisms parallel to those of the government. Where the projects have done so, it has tended to hinder the long-run enhancement of local government capacity, and thus to dilute or undermine efforts to foster decentralization and strengthen local control (IEG 2005i).

By sidelining local governments, CDD projects have often missed the opportunity to engage local officials in decision making and to enhance their capacity to identify, appraise, and supervise subprojects. Furthermore, they have missed the opportunity to strengthen local governments' ability to effectively engage with local communities and thereby increase their accountability to them. The Bank's social fund

The importance of strengthening partnerships between local governments and community groups is increasingly recognized.

project in Jamaica and CDD projects in Brazil's Northeast illustrate the risks of bypassing local governments and creating parallel structures. In Jamaica, the sustainability of investments in roads has been jeopardized by bypassing the local councils responsible for maintaining them. In Brazil, Bank-supported CDD projects in the Northeast have contributed to a proliferation of uncoordinated and ad hoc municipal councils that constitute a structure parallel to that of the planning process of municipal government (IEG 2002b, 2005i).[3]

Local governments have often been bypassed on grounds that they lack capacity. Yet Albania's experience counters this argument. Even though local governments in that country are of very recent vintage, they are key to realizing projects financed by the Albanian Development Fund. Local governments make the final decisions on subprojects to be funded, and with the fund's assistance they contract out the works through public tenders (IEG 2002b).

There is growing recognition in the Bank of the importance of building partnerships between community groups and local government organizations and of strengthening the use of local systems. For example, a recent Bank-supported social fund project in Zambia is designed to integrate into the larger decentralization effort in the country. Zambian district authorities are given increasing responsibility in the project cycle for community-level subprojects (IEG 2005i). Other social funds, such as the one in Honduras, have contributed to decentralization by helping to strengthen local government capacities in participatory budgeting, project planning, and implementation (IEG 2006l).

While support for enhancing local government capacity under CDD projects has significantly increased in recent years, the Bank has not always followed a consistent approach across different projects that aimed to foster local control within a country. This inconsistency has arisen in countries where the Bank has supported projects under different institutional arrangements.

In Senegal, for example, Bank operations were helping to build the capacity of representative local governments and communities to manage programs and raise resources. But the Bank's methods seemed inconsistent with its goal of developing strong local government.

An Urban Development and Decentralization Project in Senegal helped many urban municipalities learn how to prepare and implement investment programs and manage assets. In doing so, it created parallel institutional arrangements and financing mechanisms that bypassed the regular ones. In Senegal's rural communities, two different operations supported capacity building. One—the Rural Infrastructure Project—worked within the existing administrative framework for transfer of funds, thereby reinforcing the decentralization process. The other—the social fund—operated in many of the same rural areas, but relied on nongovernmental agencies (IEG 2006q). Recognizing the need to reconcile the different approaches used under past projects, the recently approved Participatory Local Development Project now aims at consolidating the experiences gained from the previous two projects in rural areas (World Bank 2006k).

Different projects aiming to foster local control within a country did not always use consistent approaches.

Conclusions

This ARDE has reviewed factors that affect the Bank's ability to achieve results at the country and sector levels and its efforts to help strengthen the accountability of public sector institutions responsible for country-level results. It has found several factors that can further strengthen the Bank's effectiveness in helping countries reduce poverty.

Strategies need to identify growth patterns likely to reduce poverty.

Economic growth over the past decade has led to substantial poverty reduction in many East and South Asian countries, and more recently in the transition economies of Eastern Europe and Central Asia. But the kind of growth that delivers significant poverty reduction continues to elude a considerable number of developing countries.

Sustained growth has been shown to reduce poverty better than sporadic growth. Only two in five borrowing countries have recorded continuous per capita income growth over the five years 2000–05, and just one in five did so for a full ten years, 1995–2005. High or worsening inequality has dampened the poverty-reducing effect of growth in some countries. This was particularly the case in countries where growth was concentrated in sectors that generated little employment and where the poor lacked the basic skills or mobility to take advantage of opportunities arising from growth.

Strategies aimed only at boosting overall growth may miss opportunities to reduce poverty effectively. In countries that had growth without poverty reduction, IEG found that growth was concentrated in subsectors that created little employment. The Bank's assistance in these countries often effectively contributed to bringing the countries back to a growth path through improved economic management, but it was less successful in bringing about job-creating growth.

The poor tend to live in rural areas. The Bank has found it challenging to help countries formulate and implement strategies that effectively reduce rural poverty. About half of the Country Assistance Strategy reviews carried out by IEG over the past four fiscal years concluded that the Bank's assistance in rural areas had either not led to satisfactory outcomes or that rural poverty reduction required increased attention.

To support growth strategies that more consistently translate into poverty reduction, the countries, the Bank, and their partners will need to further strengthen their understanding of what keeps the poor from participating in growth in each country, what prevents growth from reaching particular regions and sectors, and how urban-rural linkages and intersectoral mobility can be enhanced.

Achieving results requires realistic objectives.

The Bank's assistance has been effective when it has been realistic about borrowers' political and institutional capacity and has had well-specified objectives. But IEG found that almost half of all Bank Country Assistance Strategies it examined over the past four fiscal years were overly ambitious in two distinct ways. They either lacked selectivity or they were founded on unrealistic expectations for a reform program that was not commensurate with the institutional capacity and political situation in the client country.

Strategies that lacked selectivity caused the Bank's programs to spread their resources too thinly across too many sectors, which diminished the impact of individual operations. Strategies that were based on unrealistic expectations for reform programs led the Bank to proceed with policy-based lending, even when country conditions were not fully ready for the targeted reforms.

Unrealistic goals are also found in individual lending operations. For instance, many financial sector loans in crisis countries have had unduly ambitious objectives, driven by overestimation of the government's commitment to reform and a need to justify large loans. At the same time, Country Assistance Evaluations have also shown that realistic and well-defined objectives can produce results when stakeholders are focused on them.

Achieving sector-level impact requires more than satisfactory project outcomes.

The performance of the Bank's portfolio has improved over the past five fiscal years. Over three-quarters of Bank-financed operations achieved a moderately satisfactory or better outcome rating during this period.

However, Country Assistance Evaluations show that satisfactory project outcomes alone do not ensure country-sector impact. It is careful selection and phasing of interventions; long-term engagement; and the complementarities of lending, analytical work, and policy dialogue that lead to impact on the sector as a whole.

Bank-financed operations have yielded good results when they have supported a country-formulated, broadly owned sector strategy with clear objectives, and when they have followed a distinct pathway designed to reach milestones that contributed to the achievement of the country's objectives for the sector.

Balancing long-term and short-term goals improves results.

Achieving high-quality development results takes time, but pressure to show results quickly can divert attention from the quality of results. For instance, the Millennium Development Goal of ensuring universal completion of primary education by 2015 has spurred massive efforts to increase school enrollment. This is good, as long as rapid expansion in coverage does not come at the expense of attention to learning outcomes. In many countries, however, the rapid expansion did affect the learning environment, and only about one-third of primary education sector operations assessed by IEG explicitly aimed to improve learning outcomes.

In post-conflict countries, the pressure to show quick results is especially intense, but haste may lead to the neglect of the institution building that is vital for recovery. The long time required to reach many of the intended results underscores the importance of continuity of Bank engagement and of defining what is feasible for a single operation to achieve. A judicious combination of longer-term objectives with interventions that yield quick and visible results has been found effective.

Strong results demand attention to cross-sectoral synergies.

Achieving results in a given sector often requires identifying and removing constraints in other sectors as well. The countries and the Bank need to pay more attention to these complementary effects. The impact of infrastructure investments financed by community development projects, for example, has often been diminished by lack of attention to inputs such as teachers, doctors, and medicines. Similarly, Bank-supported pension reforms have at times not achieved the desired results because insufficient attention was given to ensuring that the necessary macroeconomic, financial, and institutional conditions were in place. The Bank's matrix management structure does not provide staff with sufficient incentives to work across sectoral boundaries and address cross-sectoral issues.

More attention is also needed to the distributional impact of reforms supported by the Bank at the country level, because not all pro-growth policies are distributionally neutral. In the area of trade reform, for example, the Bank often failed to conduct sufficient analysis to inform its policy advice and lending about the employment and poverty effects of reforms. A proper assessment of the distributional impact of proposed reforms in a particular country often requires analysis that reaches beyond the sector in which the reforms are carried out.

Even though achieving a particular sector goal may require a multisectoral approach, large multisector operations are not always an effective way to achieve sectoral results. The sectoral impact of multisector operations has tended to be weaker than that of sector-specific operations, partly because multisector operations allow for less-intensive engagement of Bank sector teams with country line agencies. In the financial sector, for example, the outcome of loans overseen by Bank financial sector departments was substantially better than that of financial sector components of multisector loans. Similarly, pension-specific loans and pension reform components of development policy lending operations led by the social protection and financial sector departments have achieved better outcomes than pension components of multisector operations led by economic policy teams. A combination of policy-based lending (which is often multisectoral) and sector-specific operations can deliver good results.

Large-scale public sector reforms require political commitment.

Achieving and maintaining results requires public sector institutions that are accountable to stakeholders. For this reason, Bank Country Assistance Strategies emphasize strengthening the performance and accountability of the public sector.

The bulk of the Bank's support has taken the form of reform programs in public administration and public financial management. This assistance has led to improved processes in some countries, but it has not yet translated into improvements in the perceived quality of governance in most of them. Yet experience in a few countries shows that it is possible to make progress rapidly when there is strong country commitment to do so.

Evaluations suggest that reform initiatives have not always been aligned with political circumstances. They have focused on new legislation and institutions, while overlooking enforcement. They have also tended to overlook the interface between the private and the public sectors, even though regulatory reforms have often been shown to be effective against corruption.

Many reform programs have been undermined by lack of political support. The extent of political opposition is often underestimated at the time of program design. Even reforms of a "technocratic" nature, such as those of civil service personnel practices, can succeed only when they build on political commitment. When political conditions are not ready for reforms, IEG has found it advisable to proceed gradually, identifying opportunities for less contentious reforms in order to build momentum.

Regulatory reform can help curb corruption.

The interface between the private and public sectors is fertile ground both for corruption and for combating it. Reforms to regulatory regimes have made headway against corruption even when they have not been part of comprehensive anticorruption programs. Such sector-specific opportunities to combat corruption need to be more systematically exploited in Bank operations.

Transparency and local control encourage the public sector to deliver.

Transparency is the foundation of good governance because access to information reduces corruption, and transparent institutions earn the public's trust. Bank operations have helped bring more transparency to a variety of public management processes, including budget formulation and execution, procurement, and customs administration.

Local control and community participation can make public sector institutions more accountable. Bank operations support such local control in two main ways: by upgrading local government agencies and by channeling resources directly to communities. But community-driven development projects can also dilute efforts to foster decentralization when they establish structures parallel to those of local government. There is now growing recognition in the Bank of the importance of strengthening the use of local systems in the course of promoting community development.

Future directions

This ARDE finds three important areas where the Bank can further strengthen its effectiveness in helping countries reduce poverty.

- *A focus on the nature of growth.* Poverty reduction will continue to require a strong focus on growth. To ensure that growth translates efficiently into poverty reduction, however, the countries, the Bank, and their partners will need to find effective ways to enhance the ability of the poor to participate in this growth. This will require country-level analysis of the binding constraints to employment-creating growth and to growth in regions where the poor may be concentrated, as well as analysis of the factors that hinder the intersectoral mobility of the poor.

- *A well-articulated results chain to achieve sectoral outcomes.* A well-articulated results chain allows Bank operations to ensure that objectives are set realistically, that cross-sectoral constraints to achieving them are adequately considered, and that due attention is given to capacity building, particularly when the Bank's assistance focuses on policy-based lending. Effective articulation and utilization of the results chain also requires efforts to enhance country capacity to collect and use performance information.

- *A realistic assessment of the political economy of governance-related reforms.* The Bank can provide countries with the tools needed to strengthen government processes, and thereby to improve the governance environment, but effective use of those tools remains in the hands of country decision makers. Thus, reforms to improve the accountability of public sector institutions require broad-based political support. When such support is absent, an incremental approach that allows momentum for reforms to build can help deliver results. These reforms can be further enhanced with continued efforts to foster local demand for accountability through increased transparency of government processes.

APPENDIXES

APPENDIX A: PROJECT PERFORMANCE RESULTS

This appendix presents long-term trends in project performance based on IEG project evaluations. Consistent with past ARDEs, the appendix uses the year 1990 as a starting point in analyzing long-term trends. Following a brief description of the cohort of recent IEG project evaluations, analysis of the Bank's lending effectiveness is presented for each of IEG's three key performance criteria: outcome, sustainability, and institutional development impact.

Composition of the ARDE 2006 Exiting Cohort

IEG has evaluated 502 closed projects since the last ARDE; 82 percent of these exited the Bank's portfolio during fiscal 2004 and 2005.[1] These evaluations cover US$33.6 billion in disburse-

ments and consist of 410 ICR Reviews and 92 Project Performance Assessment Reports (PPARs).[2] This newly evaluated cohort consists of 89 development policy lending operations and 412 investment operations, the vintage of which is shown in figure A.1.[3] The data for fiscal 2005 exits represent a partial cohort of lending exits (274 out of 317).

Performance Trends
Outcome

Projects in exit fiscal year 2004 registered an increase in performance outcome,[4] which jumped from 74 percent to 78 percent satisfactory between fiscal 2003 and 2004, as shown in figure A.2. Project performance in exit fiscal 2004 exceeded the Strategic Compact target of 75

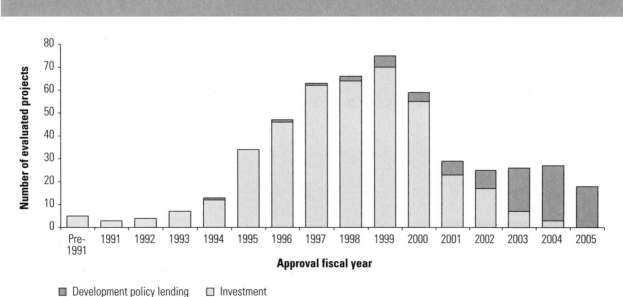

Figure A.1: ARDE 2006 Exiting Cohort by Approval Year

■ Development policy lending   □ Investment

Source: World Bank database.

Figure A.2: Project Performance Continues to Meet Strategic Compact Target

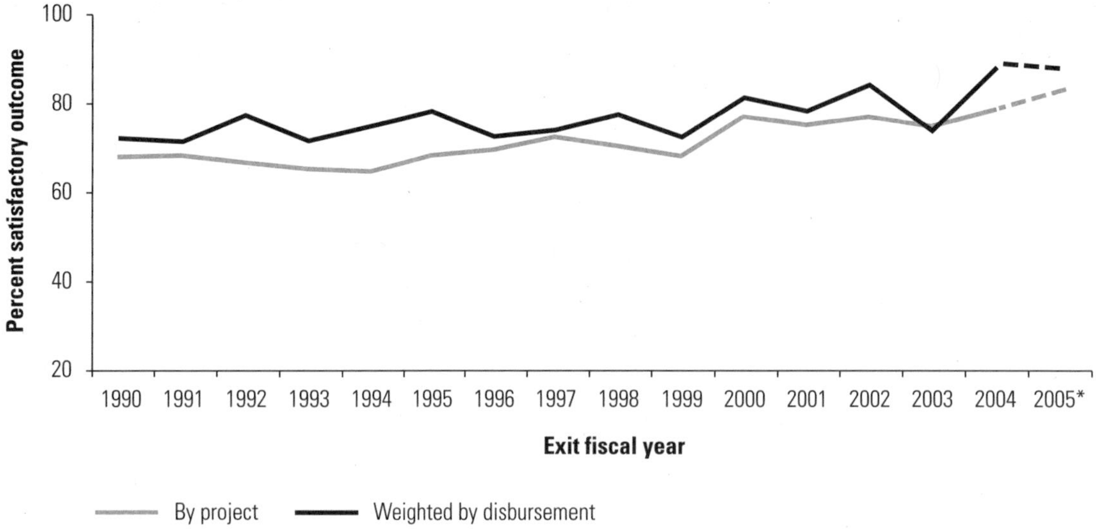

Source: World Bank database.

Note: 2005 data are partial (dashed line).

percent satisfactory outcomes, which had not been met by exit fiscal 2003 projects.

IEG had evaluated 82 percent of the 317 fiscal 2005 exits as of September 15, 2006. For this partial fiscal 2005 cohort,[5] outcome is rated satisfactory for 82 percent of projects, and for 87 percent weighted by disbursements. This represents a significant recovery from the fiscal 2003 drop and a return to improved results that began in fiscal 2000.

Sustainability and institutional development impact

Eighty-eight percent (weighted by disbursements) of the exit fiscal 2004 cohort are rated "likely" or "highly likely" to be resilient to future risks.[6] The fiscal 2004 rating for sustainability marks a significant increase from the fiscal 2003 cohort rating of 73 percent and represents a return to the upward trend that began in 1996. For the fiscal 2005 (partial) cohort, sustainability ratings weighted by disbursements continued to improve, increasing to 90 percent.

Sixty-eight percent (weighted by disbursements) of the fiscal 2004 cohort are rated to have a substantial or high institutional development impact.[7] The institutional development impact rating represents a significant increase over the fiscal 2003 cohort rating of 48 percent. For the fiscal 2005 (partial) cohort, institutional development impact modestly decreased to 64 percent (disbursement weighted) substantial or better. Notwithstanding this modest decline, both sustainability and institutional development impact ratings represented, at a minimum, a 15-percentage-point increase for the fiscal 2005 (partial) cohort over the fiscal 2003 cohort. As with outcome ratings, these improvements may indicate a resumption of the upward trend in project performance (figure A.3).

Regional performance

Figure A.4 presents the percentage of satisfactory project outcomes, weighted by disbursement, for the fiscal 2001–05 (partial) cohort compared with the fiscal 1996–2000 cohort. The East Asia and Pacific, Middle East and North Africa, Europe and Central Asia, and South Asia Regions are the top performers for the fiscal 2001–05 (partial) cohort, exceeding the Bank average of 81 percent. The Latin America and Caribbean Region, which was the best performer

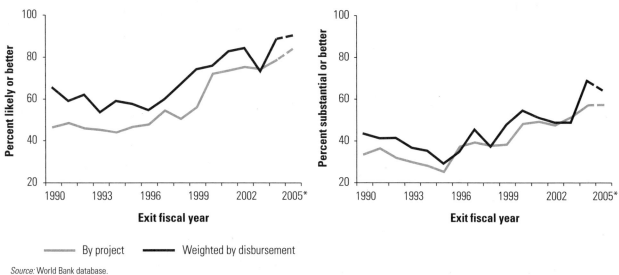

Figure A.3: Long-Term Trends in Sustainability and Institutional Development

100
80
60
40
20
Percent likely or better
1990
1993
1996
1999
2002
2005*
Exit fiscal year
Percent substantial or better
Exit fiscal year
By project
Weighted by disbursement

Source: World Bank database.

Note: 2005 data are partial (dashed line).

for the fiscal 1996–2000 cohort, is the only one that declined in performance for the fiscal 2000–05 (partial) cohort. The Africa Region improved in performance for fiscal 2000–05, but was below the Bank average in both periods and continues to lag behind all other Regions. The Europe and Central Asia and South Asia Regions made the most progress in outcome perform-

Figure A.4: Projects Improved in All but One Region

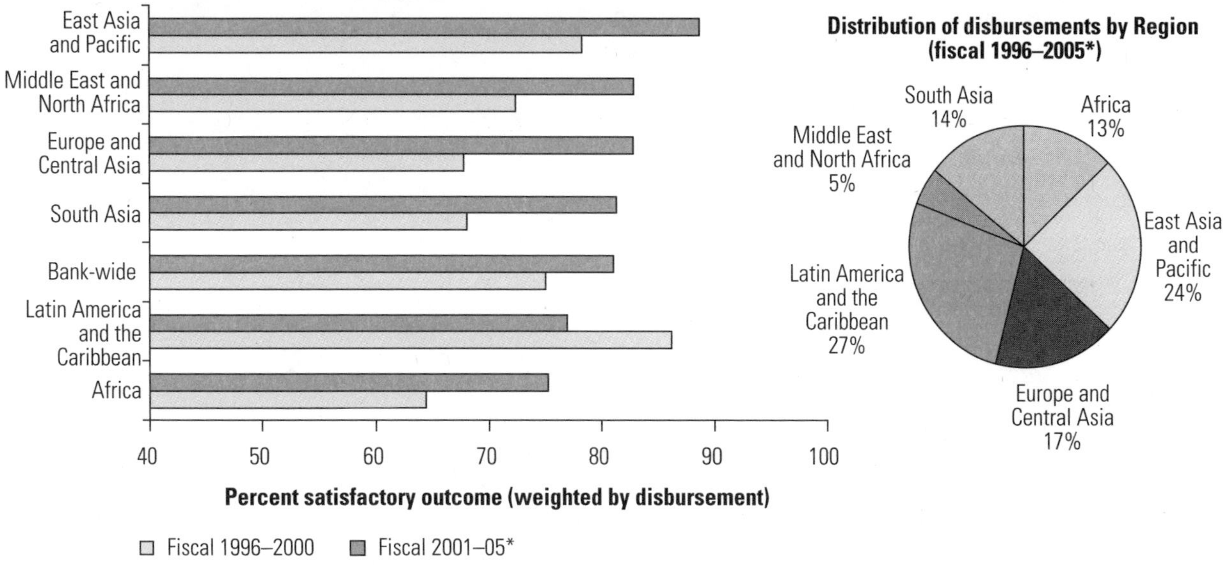

East Asia and Pacific
Middle East and North Africa
Europe and Central Asia
South Asia
Bank-wide
Latin America and the Caribbean
Africa
40
50
60
70
80
90
100
Percent satisfactory outcome (weighted by disbursement)
Fiscal 1996–2000
Fiscal 2001–05*
Distribution of disbursements by Region (fiscal 1996–2005*)
South Asia 14%
Africa 13%
Middle East and North Africa 5%
East Asia and Pacific 24%
Latin America and the Caribbean 27%
Europe and Central Asia 17%

Source: World Bank database.

Note: 2005* data are partial.

ance, improving by 15 and 13 percentage points, respectively.

Sectoral performance

Compared with the fiscal 1996–2000 cohort, the outcome performance weighted by disbursement for the fiscal 2001–05 (partial) cohort improved in 10 of 14 sector boards.[8] Figure A.5 presents the sector boards' outcome performance in order of improvement. The biggest improvements in outcome ratings were in energy and mining, environment, water supply and sanitation, and the financial sector. The largest declines in performance were in the social protection sector and in health, nutrition, and population. Outcomes for economic policy and water supply and sanitation were below the Bank-wide average in both periods.

Lending instrument performance

Outcomes of development policy lending operations rebounded in fiscal 2004, registering a significant improvement to 94 percent from a low of 71 percent in fiscal 2003. As figure A.6 shows, outcomes (disbursement-weighted) of development policy lending have fluctuated in recent years. However, exit fiscal 2005 (partial), at a high disbursement-weighted performance

Figure A.5: Trends in Sectoral Performance

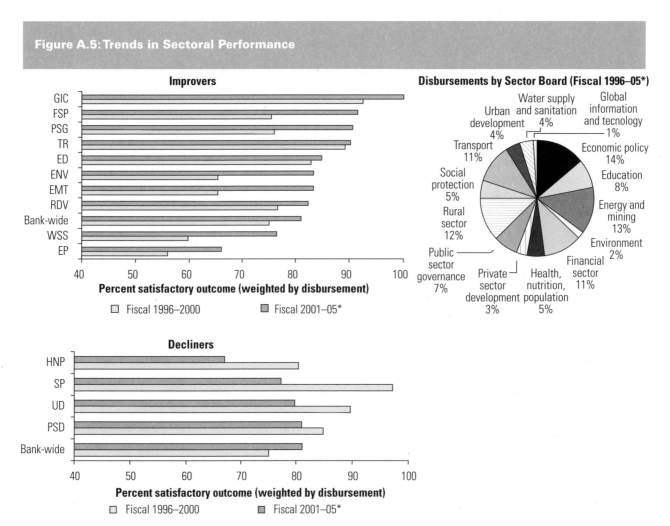

Source: World Bank database.

Note: 2005* data are partial. The sector board classification applies to the whole project and enables outcomes to be matched to it.

Key: EP = economic policy; ED = education; EMT = energy and mining; ENV = environment; FSP = financial sector; GIC = global information and technology; HNP = health, nutrition, and population; PSD = private sector development; PSG = public sector governance; RDV = rural sector; SP = social protection; TR = transport; UD = urban development; WSS = water supply and sanitation.

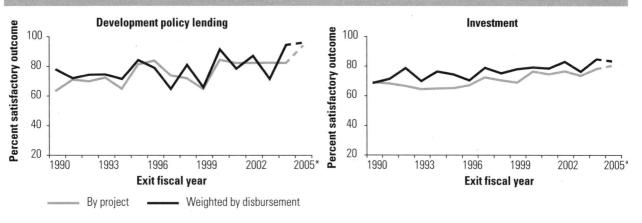

Figure A.6: Long-Term Trends in Development Policy and Investment Lending °

Source: World Bank database.

Note: 2005* data are partial (dashed line).

of 96 percent, shows that outcome ratings for development policy lending operations may be on a steady improvement trend.

New lending instruments

IEG has evaluated 172 operations employing the Bank's four new lending instruments—Adaptable Program Loans (APLs), Learning and Innovation Loans (LILs), Programmatic Sector Adjustment Loans (PSALs), and Poverty Reduction Support Credits (PRSCs).[9] All but two of these operations exited the Bank's portfolio during the fiscal 2001–05 (partial) period, amounting to $12.6 billion in disbursements, and accounting for 12 percent of all the projects

and 13 percent of all the disbursements that exited during that period.

For these instruments, in the aggregate, outcome is rated satisfactory for 82 percent of projects, and 95 percent weighted by disbursements, exceeding the Bank-wide averages of 77 percent and 81 percent, respectively (figure A.7). PRSCs and PSALs are the best performers of the group, exceeding the Bank averages for both projects and disbursement-weighted. APLs, while exceeding the Bank average for projects, are performing below the Bank average for disbursement-weighted, while LILs are performing below the Bank average across the board.

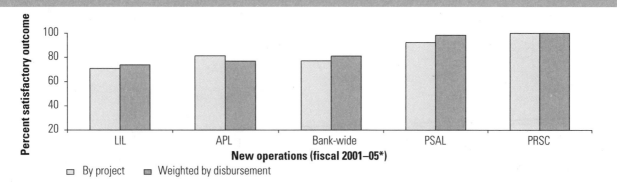

Figure A.7: Outcome Performance of New Lending Instruments

Source: World Bank database.

Note: LIL = Learning and Innovation Loan; APL = Adaptable Program Loan; PSAL = Programmatic Sector Adjustment Loan; PRSC = Poverty Reduction Support Credit.

Table A.1: Outcome, Sustainability, and Institutional Development (ID) Impact by Various Dimensions, by Project, Fiscal 1996–2005*

	Exit fiscal year 1996–2000				
	Number of projects	Share (%)	Outcome (% satisfactory)	Sustainability (% likely or better)	ID impact (% substantial or better)
Sector board					
Economic policy	96	7.3	65.6	63.4	32.3
Educaton	114	8.6	77.2	55.0	29.8
Energy and mining	154	11.7	63.2	52.3	38.8
Environment	55	4.2	72.7	66.7	41.8
Financial sector	79	6.0	62.3	56.0	42.1
Global information/ communications technology	21	1.6	81.0	76.2	57.1
Health, nutrition, and population	77	5.8	64.9	52.6	35.1
Poverty reduction	0	0.0	0.0	0.0	0.0
Private sector development	62	4.7	70.5	60.7	28.3
Public sector governance	86	6.5	78.6	75.0	47.6
Rural sector	253	19.2	65.7	45.3	39.6
Social development	0	0.0	0.0	0.0	0.0
Social protection	66	5.0	86.2	50.0	52.3
Transport	127	9.6	86.1	67.8	56.6
Urban development	67	5.1	77.3	51.5	33.3
Water supply and sanitation	63	4.8	59.7	41.9	27.4
Overall result	*1,320*	*100.0*	*71.0*	*55.8*	*39.7*
Lending instrument type					
Development policy lending	193	14.6	74.6	69.0	43.2
Investment	1,126	85.3	70.3	53.5	39.1
Not assigned	1	0.1	0.0	100.0	0.0
Overall result	*1,320*	*100.0*	*71.0*	*55.8*	*39.7*
Network					
Environmentally & socially sustainable development	308	23.3	67.0	49.2	40.0
Financial sector	79	6.0	62.3	56.0	42.1
Human development	257	19.5	75.8	53.0	37.1
Infrastructure	432	32.7	72.3	56.3	42.3
Poverty reduction & economic management	182	13.8	71.7	68.8	39.4
Private sector development	62	4.7	70.5	63.9	28.3
Overall result	*1,320*	*100.0*	*71.0*	*55.8*	*39.7*
Region					
Africa	385	29.2	57.3	38.9	32.4
East Asia and Pacific	195	14.8	78.6	62.6	44.0
Europe and Central Asia	214	16.2	80.5	73.2	50.5
Latin America and the Caribbean	273	20.7	79.3	63.1	45.7
Middle East and North Africa	102	7.7	69.3	55.0	30.7
South Asia	151	11.4	69.3	54.1	33.3
Overall result	*1,320*	*100.0*	*71.0*	*55.8*	*39.7*

	Exit fiscal year 2001–05*					Exit fiscal year 1996–2005*			
Number of projects	Share (%)	Outcome (% satisfactory)	Sustainability (% likely or better)	ID impact (% substantial or better)	Number of projects	Share (%)	Outcome (% satisfactory)	Sustainability (% likely or better)	ID impact (% substantial or better)
80.0	5.7	77.2	75.0	40.5	176	6.4	70.9	68.2	36.0
146	10.3	83.4	82.3	58.3	260	9.5	80.7	69.7	45.7
102	7.2	76.8	81.1	63.6	256	9.4	68.5	63.1	48.6
81	5.7	71.8	73.6	51.9	136	5.0	72.2	70.6	47.8
70	5.0	79.4	90.2	66.2	149	5.4	70.3	71.3	53.5
13	0.9	100.0	100.0	46.2	34	1.2	88.2	84.4	52.9
122	8.6	65.5	71.1	48.7	199	7.3	65.3	63.7	43.4
9	0.6	100.0	100.0	44.4	9	0.3	100.0	100.0	44.4
78	5.5	61.8	70.8	42.7	140	5.1	65.7	66.1	36.3
118	8.3	75.4	77.8	49.2	204	7.5	76.7	76.6	48.5
222	15.7	80.0	72.9	52.6	475	17.4	72.3	57.3	45.6
13	0.9	66.7	70.0	41.7	13	0.5	66.7	70.0	41.7
92	6.5	78.3	69.7	44.6	158	5.8	81.5	60.0	47.8
122	8.6	87.6	84.9	63.6	249	9.1	86.8	75.8	60.1
80	5.7	73.4	68.0	38.0	147	5.4	75.2	60.3	35.9
66	4.7	76.9	74.6	50.8	129	4.7	68.5	57.9	39.4
1,414	100.0	77.1	76.7	52.1	2,734	100.0	74.1	66.1	46.1
205	14.5	84.2	86.5	51.0	398	14.6	79.5	77.5	47.2
1,208	85.4	75.8	75.0	52.2	2,334	85.4	73.2	64.1	45.9
1	0.1	0.0	100.0	100.0	2	0.1	0.0	100.0	50.0
1,414	100	77.1	76.7	52.1	2,734	100	74.1	66.1	46.1
316	23.3	77.4	73.0	52.0	624	22.8	72.2	60.5	46.0
70	6.0	79.4	90.2	66.2	149	5.4	70.3	71.3	53.5
360	19.5	76.1	75.5	51.5	617	22.6	76.0	65.4	45.5
383	32.7	80.4	78.9	55.4	815	29.8	76.1	66.4	48.5
207	13.8	77.2	77.7	45.6	389	14.2	74.6	73.3	42.7
78	4.7	61.8	67.6	42.7	140	5.1	65.7	66.7	36.3
1,414	100.0	77.1	76.7	52.1	2,734	100.0	74.1	66.1	46.1
349	24.7	69.4	63.8	44.2	734	26.8	63.0	49.9	37.9
217	15.3	77.7	76.2	56.3	412	15.1	78.1	69.4	50.5
303	21.4	82.4	87.6	58.3	517	18.9	81.6	81.3	55.0
296	20.9	79.8	79.0	59.4	569	20.8	79.6	71.0	52.8
126	8.9	75.8	73.9	36.3	228	8.3	72.9	64.9	33.8
123	8.7	79.7	83.8	50.4	274	10.0	74.0	66.4	41.0
1,414	100	77.1	76.7	52.1	2,734	100	74.1	66.1	46.1

Table A.2: Outcome, Sustainability, and Institutional Development (ID) Impact by Various Dimensions, by Disbursement, Fiscal 1996–2005*

	Exit fiscal year 1996–2000				
	Number of projects	Share (%)	Outcome (% satisfactory)	Sustainability (% likely or better)	ID impact (% substantial or better)
Sector board					
Economic policy	13,610	13.1	56.0	75.5	39.7
Educaton	7,108	6.8	82.9	64.4	36.1
Energy and mining	16,476	15.8	65.3	57.0	41.9
Environment	1,263	1.2	69.0	61.4	38.9
Financial sector	14,249	13.7	75.4	73.3	41.5
Global information/ communications technology	1,150	1.1	92.4	94.3	65.4
Health, nutrition, and population	4,134	4.0	80.4	68.4	42.7
Poverty reduction	0	0.0	0.0	0.0	0.0
Private sector development	3,442	3.3	84.9	75.8	42.2
Public sector governance	4,899	4.7	76.0	78.0	46.8
Rural sector	12,903	12.4	76.6	55.4	48.4
Social development	0	0.0	0.0	0.0	0.0
Social protection	4,833	4.6	97.2	72.6	54.7
Transport	11,012	10.6	89.2	70.1	57.9
Urban development	4,715	4.5	89.7	63.1	30.4
Water supply and sanitation	4,493	4.3	59.7	35.0	20.7
Overall result	*104,286*	*100.0*	*75.0*	*66.0*	*43.4*
Lending instrument type					
Development policy lending	35,612	34.1	74.0	79.7	44.9
Investment	68,674	65.9	75.5	59.2	42.6
Not assigned	0	0.0	0.0	0.0	0.0
Overall result	*104,286*	*100.0*	*75.0*	*66.0*	*43.4*
Network					
Environmentally & socially sustainable development	14,166	13.6	75.9	55.9	47.5
Financial sector	14,249	13.7	75.4	73.3	41.5
Human development	16,074	15.4	86.6	67.9	43.4
Infrastructure	37,846	36.3	75.4	60.0	43.3
Poverty reduction & economic management	18,509	17.7	61.3	77.6	41.6
Private sector development	3,442	3.3	84.9	75.8	42.2
Overall result	*104,286*	*100.0*	*75.0*	*66.0*	*43.4*
Region					
Africa	13,448	12.9	64.4	45.4	33.6
East Asia and Pacific	28,405	27.2	78.3	76.1	46.2
Europe and Central Asia	15,813	15.2	67.7	72.6	46.0
Latin America and the Caribbean	25,562	24.5	86.2	69.1	54.0
Middle East and North Africa	5,905	5.7	72.3	49.8	33.9
South Asia	15,154	14.5	68.0	60.8	30.5
Overall result	*104,286*	*100.0*	*75.0*	*66.0*	*43.4*

	Exit fiscal year 2001–05*					Exit fiscal year 1996–2005*			
Number of projects	Share (%)	Outcome (% satisfactory)	Sustainability (% likely or better)	ID impact (% substantial or better)	Number of projects	Share (%)	Outcome (% satisfactory)	Sustainability (% likely or better)	ID impact (% substantial or better)
12,479	12.7	66.0	60.8	26.5	26,090	12.9	60.8	68.7	33.4
8,957	9.1	84.9	92.7	65.4	16,065	7.9	84.0	79.7	52.4
10,156	10.4	83.4	83.3	64.4	26,632	13.2	72.2	66.9	50.4
2,781	2.8	64.1	79.9	41.4	4,044	2.0	65.9	74.1	40.6
8,661	8.8	91.5	96.4	74.9	22,910	11.3	81.5	80.8	56.0
855	0.9	100.0	100.0	57.5	2,005	1.0	95.7	96.7	62.0
6,308	6.4	67.0	77.6	55.3	10,442	5.2	72.3	73.9	50.3
662	0.7	100.0	100.0	33.5	662	0.3	100.0	100.0	33.5
3,243	3.3	81.0	89.1	73.7	6,685	3.3	83.0	82.2	57.4
8,967	9.2	90.6	91.2	52.8	13,866	6.9	85.4	87.3	50.7
11,144	11.4	82.4	79.5	59.2	24,047	11.9	79.3	66.6	53.5
405	0.4	29.8	92.1	22.2	405	0.2	29.8	92.1	22.2
4,788	4.9	77.3	81.9	52.4	9,621	4.8	87.3	76.8	53.6
10,874	11.1	90.2	91.6	59.5	21,885	10.8	89.7	80.1	58.7
4,131	4.2	79.8	73.3	40.6	8,846	4.4	85.1	67.8	35.2
3,581	3.7	76.4	70.6	50.9	8,074	4.0	67.1	50.6	34.1
97,994	*100.0*	*81.1*	*82.6*	*54.9*	*202,281*	*100.0*	*77.9*	*73.7*	*49.1*
36,490	37.2	82.3	83.2	51.6	72,102	35.6	78.2	81.4	48.4
61,504	62.8	80.3	82.2	56.9	130,179	64.4	77.8	69.7	49.4
0	0.0	0.0	0.0	0.0	0	0.0	0.0	0.0	0.0
97,994	*100.0*	*81.1*	*82.6*	*54.9*	*202,281*	*100.0*	*77.9*	*73.7*	*49.1*
14,330	14.6	77.8	79.9	54.7	28,497	14.1	76.9	68.0	51.2
8,661	8.8	91.5	96.4	74.9	22,910	11.3	81.5	80.8	56.0
20,053	20.5	77.4	85.3	59.1	36,128	17.9	81.5	77.2	52.1
29,597	30.2	85.0	83.6	57.4	67,442	33.3	79.6	70.0	49.5
22,109	22.6	77.0	74.5	37.4	40,618	20.1	69.8	76.0	39.3
3,243	3.3	81.0	89.1	73.7	6,685	3.3	83.0	82.2	57.4
97,994	*100.0*	*81.1*	*82.6*	*54.9*	*202,281*	*100.0*	*77.9*	*73.7*	*49.1*
13,200	13.5	75.2	70.2	41.9	26,648	13.2	69.8	57.0	37.7
19,678	20.1	88.7	88.3	69.6	48,083	23.8	82.5	81.1	56.4
17,782	18.1	82.8	91.9	63.0	33,594	16.6	75.7	82.4	55.0
28,545	29.1	76.9	75.1	52.3	54,107	26.7	81.4	72.2	53.1
4,955	5.1	82.8	85.4	36.3	10,860	5.4	77.1	65.7	35.0
13,833	14.1	81.3	88.6	48.3	28,987	14.3	74.3	73.2	39.0
97,994	*100.0*	*81.1*	*82.6*	*54.9*	*202,281*	*100.0*	*77.9*	*73.7*	*49.1*

APPENDIX B: SECTOR AND PROJECT OUTCOME RATINGS IN COUNTRY ASSISTANCE EVALUATIONS

This appendix presents the sector outcomes and corresponding project outcomes of 18 countries based on a review of each country's Country Assistance Evaluation (CAE), completed by IEG in fiscal 2004–06 (table B.1).

Not all CAEs covered all sectors, and the sectoral outcome ratings are based on CAEs that either had an explicit sectoral outcome rating assigned by the CAE task team leader or had sufficient sectoral information for the ARDE team to make an assessment in consultation with the original CAE task team leader. The

project outcome ratings are based on projects that were included in the CAE and targeted the relevant sectors. Columns I & IV represent countries that had both satisfactory sector and project outcomes and both unsatisfactory sector and project outcomes, respectively. Column II represents countries that had satisfactory sector outcomes while the majority of projects targeting the sector had unsatisfactory outcomes. Column III represents countries that had unsatisfactory sector outcomes while the majority of projects targeting the sector had satisfactory outcomes.

Table B.1: Sectoral and Project Outcomes for Country Assistance Evaluations Completed in Fiscal 2004–06

Sector	I Countries with satisfactory sector outcome & >=50% satisfactory project outcome (%)	II Countries with satisfactory sector outcome & <50% satisfactory project outcome (%)	III Countries with unsatisfactory sector outcome & >=50% satisfactory project outcome (%)	IV Countries with unsatisfactory sector outcome & <50% satisfactory project outcome (%)	Total number of CAEs rated
Social protection	86			14	7
Rural	43	7	50		14
Private sector development	50		33	17	12
Environment	67		33		3
Financial sector	78		22		9
Public sector governance	30		60	10	10
Infrastructure	67	8	25		12
Health	70	8		23	13
Education	69	6	13	13	16

Note: "Satisfactory sector outcome" and "satisfactory project outcome" include sectors and projects rated as moderately satisfactory, satisfactory, or highly satisfactory. Likewise, "unsatisfactory sector outcome" and "unsatisfactory project outcome" include sectors and projects rated as moderately unsatisfactory, unsatisfactory, or highly unsatisfactory.

APPENDIX C: PROJECT OUTCOMES AND POLICY AND INSTITUTIONAL QUALITY

This appendix explores whether the overall quality of client countries' policies and institutions affects the likelihood of project success.

Using ordinary least squares (OLS) regression analysis, the hypothesis is tested that policy and institutional factors affect the likelihood of a Bank project meeting its stated objective, as measured by an IEG project outcome rating of satisfactory (including projects rated moderately satisfactory, satisfactory, or highly satisfactory). The dependent variable is defined as the percentage of projects with a satisfactory outcome rating in a given country over the period fiscal 2001–05. Only countries with at least three exiting projects between fiscal 2001 and 2005 are included.

As a first step, the World Bank's Country Policy and Institutional Assessment (CPIA) ratings were used as explanatory variables, in addition to controlling for income level (ln of GDP per capita). The CPIA ratings are grouped in four clusters: economic management, structural policies, policies for social inclusion and equity, and public sector management and institutions. The regression used, for each of the four CPIA clusters, the average overall ratings for 1999–2004. The results, shown in column 1 of table C.1, suggest that economic management and policies for social inclusion both positively affect the likelihood of satisfactory project outcome. However, because of high collinearity among the four CPIA clusters, alternative specifications are used to further explore the relationship between the quality of institutions and likelihood of project outcome.

Column 3 shows the results of an alternative specification that retains the economic manage-ment component of the CPIA and adds another indicator of institutional quality, the International Country Risk Guide (ICRG) index of law and order, as well as a variable to control for external shocks, the coefficient of variation of the terms of trade index. Economic management remains a statistically significant explanatory variable, and law and order is also positively related to the likelihood of satisfactory project outcome. The variation in terms of trade, however, does not seem to affect the likelihood of project success.

Adding further explanatory variables related to governance and institutional quality, such as an indicator of perception of corruption (the ICRG index of corruption), does not improve the explanatory power of the regression much (column 4). There does not appear to be a statis-tically significant relation between the level of perceived corruption and likelihood of satisfac-tory project outcome.

Finally, adding Regional dummies for each of the World Bank's six Regions (with the Middle East and North Africa as the control Region) does not yield any additional insights. Once income per capita, the quality of economic management, and law and order are controlled for, countries in the Africa or Latin America and Caribbean Region, for example, are not any more or less likely to achieve satisfactory project outcomes than countries in other Regions. To test further for Regional differences in project success rates, various iterations of regressions were also estimated comparing each Region individually to all other borrowers. These iterations confirmed that there is no Regional difference in project outcomes once the other variables discussed above are controlled for.

Table C.1: Results of Ordinary Least Squares Regressions

	1	2	3	4	5
GDP per capita	0.00	0.01	0.01	0.01	0.00
	−0.23	−0.81	−0.57	−0.42	−0.18
Economic management	0.15	0.19	0.19	0.17	0.16
	(3.91)**	(7.62)**	(6.79)**	(5.83)**	(5.17)**
Structural policies	−0.08				
	−1.33				
Policies for Inclusion	0.16				
	(2.92)**				
Public sector management	0.01				
	−0.10				
Law and order			0.04	0.04	0.04
			(2.46)*	(2.43)*	(2.14)*
Corruption				0.04	0.05
				−1.43	−1.70
Terms of trade			0.17	0.11	0.11
			−0.83	−0.56	−0.52
Africa					−0.03
					−0.42
East Asia and the Pacific					0.10
					−1.33
Europe and Central Asia					0.02
					−0.25
Latin America and the Caribbean					0.03
					−0.46
South Asia					0.06
					−0.59
Constant	−0.14	−0.05	−0.17	−0.17	−0.09
	−1.20	−0.43	−1.40	−1.46	−0.48
Observations	106	106	77	77	77
R-squared	0.50	0.44	0.55	0.56	0.59

Note: * Significant at 5%; ** significant at 1%. Absolute value of t statistics in parentheses.

This appendix provides statistical and methodological background to the poverty-related information presented in chapter 2.

Data

The analysis is based on a sample of 25 countries for which IEG completed a Country Assistance Evaluation (CAE) or analysis of a Country Assistance Strategy Completion Report (CASCR) between fiscal 2003 and 2006 and for which comparable household survey data for at least two periods are available from Povcalnet, between the mid-1990s and the early 2000s. The data used to calculate changes in poverty reduction, income, and inequality were obtained from Povcalnet, a database managed by the World Bank's Development Research Group. This database contains data on household income and/or consumption derived from country household surveys for 82 countries, but data from 2001 onward are only available for 57 countries. For 25 of these, IEG completed a CAE or analysis of a CASCR during fiscal 2003–06 and poverty data is available for at least two years between the mid-1990s and early 2000s from Povcalnet.

Data in Povcalnet is presented in deciles of per capita consumption or income, depending on the household survey. Consumption and/or income means are converted into 1993 U.S. dollars using the Bank's purchasing power parity exchange rate. No adjustments were made for adult equivalencies.

Povcalnet also makes available an interactive computational tool that allows calculations of poverty and inequality measures from the data sets. It does this by calculating the parameters of two Lorenz curves from the consumption/income deciles, the general quadratic and the beta Lorenz curves underlying the decile consumption/income distributions. Poverty and inequality measures are then derived from these parametrizations (for further details see www.worldbank.org/povcalnet).

Table D.1 presents the survey years and poverty line used to calculate the poverty reduction performance for each country, and table D.2 shows the poverty and inequality measures thus derived.

Rural and urban poverty measures were also calculated for each country from the same data sets. However, because Povcalnet does not make data available for urban and rural regions separately, with the exception of China, the poverty measures were calculated and provided by the Development Economics Research Group (DECRG) from unit record data. Results are presented in table D.3.

Changes in poverty reduction can be attributed to changes in income and in income distribution. The relative contribution of income growth and distributional changes to poverty reduction can be derived as follows for the headcount index (Datt and Ravallion 2002):

$$H_1 - H_o = (H_1{}^* - H_o) + (H_1{}^{**} - H_o) + \text{residual}$$

where

$(H_1{}^* - H_o)$ provides the change in poverty because of a change in mean consumption/income, holding the first year Lorenz curve constant; $(H_1{}^{**} - H_o)$ provides the change in poverty because of a change in consumption/income distribution (a shift in the Lorenz curve), holding mean consumption/income of the first year constant.

Table D.1: Country Listing, Survey Years, and Poverty Line

Country	Survey dates	Poverty line
Albania	2002, 2005	$2.15/day
Armenia	1998/1999, 2003	$2.15/day
Bolivia	1997, 2002	$2.15/day
Brazil	1998, 2004	$2.15/day
Burkina Faso	1998, 2003	$1.08/day
Cameroon	1996, 2001	$1.08/day
China	1996, 2001	$2.15/day
Dominican Republic	1996, 2003	$2.15/day
Georgia	1998, 2003	$2.15/day
Honduras	1997, 2003	$2.15/day
Jordan	1997, 2002/2003	$2.15/day
Lithuania	1996, 2003	$2.15/day
Madagascar	1993, 2001	$1.08/day
Malawi	1997/1998, 2004	$1.08/day
Moldova	1998, 2003	$2.15/day
Nigeria	1996/1997, 2003	$1.08/day
Pakistan	1998/1999, 2002	$1.08/day
Peru	1996, 2002	$2.15/day
Romania	1998, 2003	$2.15/day
Senegal	1994/1995, 2001	$1.08/day
Sri Lanka	1995/1996, 2002	$1.08/day
Turkey	1994, 2003	$2.15/day
Ukraine	1996, 2003	$2.15/day
Uruguay	1998, 2003	$2.15/day
Zambia	1996, 2002/2003	$1.08/day

Note: Poverty lines: US$1.08/capita/day and US$2.15/capita/day in 1993 purchasing power parity dollars.

Table D.2: Poverty Headcount, Gini Inequality Index, and GDP per Capita Growth Rates

Country	Starting survey year	End-survey year	Poverty headcount in starting year	Poverty headcount in ending year	Gini in starting year	Gini in ending year	Annual change in poverty headcount between survey years (%)	Average annual change in GDP per capita between survey years (%)	Negative growth episodes between survey years
Albania	2002	2005	10.8	7.7	28.2	28.7	−11.3	5.1	0
Armenia	1998/99	2003	38.3	31.3	36.0	33.8	−4.4	9.8	0
Bolivia	1997	2002	39.1	42.9	58.5	60.2	1.9	0.1	1
Brazil	1998	2004	22.7	19.8	59.8	57.0	−2.3	0.7	2
Burkina Faso	1998	2003	44.9	28.7	46.9	39.6	−9.0	1.6	1
Cameroon	1996	2001	32.5	17.1	46.8	44.6	−12.8	2.4	0
China, rural	1996	2001	72.5	71.0	33.6	36.3	−0.4	7.2	0
China, urban	1996	2001	9.7	6.5	29.1	33.3	−8.0	7.2	0
Dominican Republic	1996	2003	11.7	12.0	48.7	51.9	0.4	4.2	1
Georgia	1998	2003	12.9	25.8	37.4	40.4	13.8	6.0	0
Honduras	1997	2003	30.6	36.0	53.0	53.9	2.7	0.1	1
Jordan	1997	2002/03	7.4	7.5	36.4	38.9	0.2	2.0	0
Lithuania	1996	2003	7.7	7.4	32.4	36.0	−0.5	5.7	1
Madagascar	1993	2001	46.3	61.0	46.1	47.5	3.5	0.4	3
Malawi	1997/98	2004	21.9	20.8	39.0	39.0	−0.8	0.2	2
Moldova	1998	2003	51.2	29.1	39.1	35.1	−11.3	4.6	1
Nigeria	1996/97	2003	77.9	71.0	52.0	43.6	−1.4	0.7	3
Pakistan	1998/99	2002	13.6	17.8	33.0	30.6	7.7	0.7	1
Peru	1996	2002	28.4	32.1	46.2	54.7	2.1	0.3	3
Romania	1998	2003	12.8	12.7	29.4	31.1	−0.2	4.5	1
Senegal	1994/95	2001	24.0	17.0	41.4	41.3	−5.3	1.9	0
Sri Lanka	1995/96	2002	6.6	5.8	34.4	40.2	−2.1	3.3	0
Turkey	1994	2003	18.0	19.4	41.5	43.7	0.8	1.1	2
Ukraine	1996	2003	16.4	5.0	35.1	28.1	−16.9	4.6	2
Uruguay, urban	1998	2003	4.6	7.0	45.2	44.8	8.6	−4.6	4
Zambia	1996	2002/03	72.6	76.4	49.8	42.1	0.7	0.3	1

Note: Use of per capita income/consumption and US$1.08 or US$2.15 poverty line in 1993 purchasing power parity dollars may result in poverty indices that differ from country estimates or those calculated by Bank Poverty Assessments and used in other IEG evaluations. For Honduras, for example, recent Bank analysis using consumption rather than the above-reported income-based poverty measures suggests that changes in consumption-based poverty have not been statistically significant. Estimates for some countries may also differ from estimates reported in the *World Development Indicators* because of the recent updating of the Development Economics Research Group (DECRG) poverty database or different income aggregation. The estimates reported here are based on DECRG's most recent poverty database and Povcal calculations. Data for Malawi 1997 were estimated by DECRG staff in conjunction with the Poverty Assessment rather than Povcal to ensure comparability with 2004 estimates. Data for Albania were provided by the Europe and Central Asia Region.

Table D.3: Urban/Rural Poverty Headcount

Country	Year	Rural poverty headcount	Urban poverty headcount	Year	Rural poverty headcount	Urban poverty headcount
Albania	2002	13.1	7.7	2005	10.3	4.4
Armenia	1998/99	31.8	44.7	2003	35.5	27.9
Bolivia	1997	64.7	24.0	2002	72.9	26.6
Brazil	1998	45.5	16.4	2004	37.8	16.7
Burkina Faso	1998	51.3	16.3	2003	31.8	14.2
Cameroon	1996	36.2	9.9	2001	23.9	2.6
China	1996	72.5	9.7	2001	71.0	6.5
Dominican Republic	1996	15.4	9.7	2003	16.1	10.0
Georgia	1998	10.7	13.6	2003	34.2	16.9
Honduras	1997	40.1	18.6	2003	49.4	20.1
Jordan	1997			2002/03	6.8	3.7
Malawi	1997/98			2004	23.4	6.1
Madagascar	1993			2001	69.8	35.3
Moldova	1998			2003	32.0	23.7
Nigeria	1996/97	84.0	71.2	2003	78.1	61.9
Pakistan	1998/99	16.0	7.4	2002	21.6	9.0
Peru	1996			2002	65.4	14.4
Romania	1998	19.5	7.7	2003	21.9	4.8
Senegal	1994/95	57.0	43.0	2001	51.8	48.2
Sri Lanka	1995/96			2002	5.6	0.0
Turkey	1994			2003	31.0	11.4
Ukraine	1996	9.2	21.8	2003	7.5	3.8
Uruguay	1998		4.6	2003		7.0
Zambia	1996	85.7	51.0	2002/03	82.9	64.6

Table D.4: Growth and Distribution Effects on Poverty

Country	Change in poverty due to change in mean income/consumption	Change in poverty due to change in distribution	Residual
Albania	−6.1	2.6	0.4
Armenia	−3.8	−2.5	−0.6
Bolivia	3.0	0.9	−0.1
Brazil	0.9	−3.7	0.0
Burkina Faso	−7.4	−9.2	0.4
Cameroon	−14.5	−2.5	1.7
China, rural	−2.2	0.4	0.2
China, urban	−6.9	6.0	−2.3
Dominican Republic	−1.2	1.7	−0.1
Georgia	9.2	2.3	1.3
Honduras	3.0	3.5	−1.0
Jordan	−3.3	4.6	−1.2
Lithuania	−3.4	4.7	−1.7
Madagascar	13.6	3.3	−2.1
Moldova	−17.8	−1.8	−2.5
Nigeria	−3.6	−2.3	−1.0
Pakistan	7.7	−2.9	−0.3
Peru	−5.7	9.4	0.0
Romania	−2.7	2.7	−0.1
Senegal	−7.7	0.9	−0.2
Sri Lanka	−4.1	6.1	−2.9
Turkey	−1.1	2.5	0.0
Ukraine	−3.9	−8.4	0.9
Uruguay, urban	4.1	−2.5	0.8
Zambia	4.0	−1.0	0.8

APPENDIX E: GOVERNANCE INDICATORS FOR BANK BORROWERS WITH PUBLIC SECTOR PROGRAMS

Chapter 4 noted that the bulk of the Bank's work to improve the effectiveness and accountability of public sector institutions has focused on reform programs in public administration and public financial management. Analysis of the World Bank Institute's Kaufmann, Kraay, Mastruzzi (KKM) governance perception indicators illustrated that in the vast majority of countries assessed by IEG where the Bank program included public sector reforms, KKM governance perception indicators have remained unchanged since the mid-1990s, with a 90 percent level of confidence. The results are similar when the confidence interval is relaxed to 75 percent (figure E.1). Almost all countries that show an improvement under this relaxed confidence criteria are in the Eastern Europe and Central Asia Region.

The KKM indicators, like most other currently available governance indicators, are indicators of perception. While such indicators are useful, they are subject to a substantial margin of error and must be used with caution. Therefore, it is useful to consider a range of indicators to look at perceived governance quality. To this effect, this appendix also presents alternate indicators from the International Country Risk Guide (ICRG) and from the European Bank for Reconstruction and Development (EBRD)– World Bank Business Environment and Enterprise Performance Survey (BEEPS). However, it must be noted that different indicators are based on different survey methodologies and may therefore yield results that are not strictly comparable.

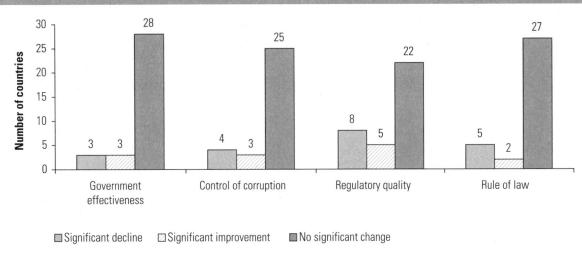

Figure E.1: Governance Perception Indicators in 35 Bank Borrowers with Public Sector Reform Programs Did Not Change Significantly Between 1996 and 2004

Source: Kaufmann, Kraay, and Mastruzzi 2005.

Note: Governance indicators are Kaufmann, Kraay, and Mastruzzi indicators between 1996 and 2004. Classification of significant changes versus no significant changes is based on a 75 percent confidence interval. Sample includes 35 countries where the Bank's assistance program included public sector reform and for which IEG completed a Country Assistance Evaluation or an analysis of a Country Assistance Strategy Completion Report in fiscal 2003–06, and for which governance indicators are available.

Figure E.2: Perceived Governance Indicators Have Not Improved Since 1996 in Selected Bank Borrowers with Public Sector Reform Programs

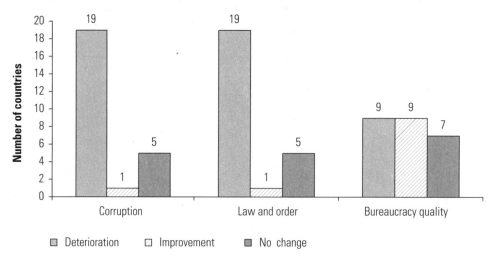

Source: International Country Risk Guide, 2006.

Note: Sample includes 35 countries where the Bank's assistance program included public sector reform and governance activities and for which IEG completed a Country Assistance Evaluation or an analysis of a CAS Completion Report in fiscal 2003–06. ICRG indicators are available for 25 of the 35 countries. Changes over time may not be statistically significant.

Figure E.3: Indicators from the Business Environment Surveys Suggest Some Improvement in Governance in Selected Transition Economies Between 2002 and 2005

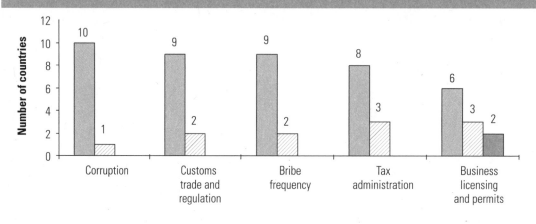

Source: World Bank 2006b.

Note: Sample includes 35 countries where the Bank's assistance program included public sector reform and governance activities and for which IEG completed a Country Assistance Evaluation or an analysis of a CAS Completion Report in fiscal 2003–06 and for which BEEPS indicators are available. BEEPS indicators are available for 11 of the 35 countries. Changes over time may not be statistically significant.

Figure E.4: The Average Quality of Budget and Financial Management Has Modestly Improved in IDA-Only Countries

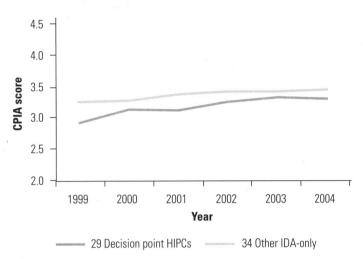

Source: World Bank CPIA database.

Note: Sample includes 29 HIPCs that had reached decision point under the initiative as of August 2006.

The bureaucracy quality, corruption, and law and order components of the ICRG's political risk category for the same country group also suggest that governance perception has not improved, and at times has even deteriorated, since the mid-1990s (figure E.2). ICRG indicators are only available for 25 of the 35 countries. In the absence of information to construct confidence intervals, the ICRG analysis was carried out using a count of sign changes from 1996 to 2005, irrespective of statistical significance. Thus, changes presented below may not be statistically significant.

The BEEPS indicators are based on surveys carried out in countries in Central Asia and Eastern Europe and the former Soviet Union. There are BEEPS data for 11 of the 35 countries assessed by IEG where the Bank supported

public sector reform through lending. These indicators, which reflect reported firm behavior rather than more broad-based governance perception, suggest an improvement in selected governance areas between 2002 and 2005 in a number of countries (figure E.3). However, these changes, too, may not be statistically significant.

Chapter 4 also finds that, on average, the quality of public expenditure management has improved modestly in 29 countries that have qualified for debt relief under HIPC, as measured by an increase in the average CPIA score for the quality of their budget and financial management (figure E.4). The quality of public expenditure management has also increased in 34 other IDA-only countries. Did HIPC countries improve their CPIA scores in this area signifi-

Table E.1: Sign Test for Change in CPIA Scores from 1999 to 2004 for Quality of Budget and Financial Management in 29 HIPC Countries

Number of countries	Number of countries with increased ratings (I)	Probability of an increase used in null hypothesis (p)	Maximum probability of observing I or more increases if probability of an increase is <=p
29	16	0.44 (15/34)	0.16

Source: World Bank CPIA database, author's calculations.

cantly more than other IDA-only countries? A sign test indicates that the tendency for HIPC countries' CPIA scores to increase was somewhat higher than it was for other IDA countries at a 84 percent confidence level, but not at a 90 percent confidence level (table E.1).

Sixteen of 29 HIPC countries posted an increase in their CPIA score for budget and financial management, while 15 of 34 non-HIPC IDA countries did so. The sign test is calculated with the null hypothesis that the differences in score between 1999 and 2004 are distributed as binomial, with the probability of an increase for HIPC countries equal to 0.44 (that is the probability of an increase in the 34 comparator IDA-only countries). The probability of getting 16 or more positive differences if the probability of a positive difference were 0.44 or less is 0.156. Therefore, it can be concluded that HIPC countries were more likely to post an improvement in the CPIA for budget and financial management than non-HIPC IDA countries at an 84 percent confidence level.

APPENDIX F: MANAGEMENT RESPONSE

Introduction

This year's *Annual Review of Development Effectiveness* (ARDE) looks at issues around growth strategies and sustainable results. In the review, the Bank's Independent Evaluation Group (IEG) discusses the Bank's recent record on growth and poverty reduction, using evaluation findings to comment on the effectiveness of World Bank assistance in contributing to poverty-reducing growth. The review groups lessons around poverty-reducing strategies, achieving results at the sector level, and strengthening public sector governance through government commitment, accountability, and transparency. This note provides a brief response to IEG's findings and suggestions. It is organized around two main issues: (a) developing countries' recent record on growth and poverty reduction; and (b)

management's views on IEG's analysis of measures that could increase the effectiveness of Bank-supported programs. In general, management finds many of IEG's suggestions to be useful as the Bank refines its efforts to support countries in improving their development effectiveness, but believes that the report could have presented a more balanced picture of Bank contributions.

Record on Growth and Poverty Reduction

The ARDE paints a relatively bleak picture on growth and poverty reduction. Management would like to note that for several years developing countries have enjoyed very positive growth rates. Figure F.1 illustrates the point, noting the recent narrowing of the gap between developing and industrial countries. Developing

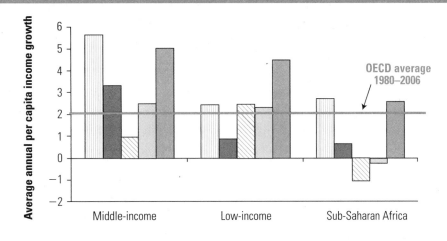

Figure F.1: Convergence: Narrowing Gap Between OECD and Developing Countries

□ 1960s ■ 1970s □ 1980s □ 1990s ■ 2001/6

Source: World Bank.

Note: OECD = Organisation for Economic Co-operation and Development.

countries grew at 5–6 percent in 2004–06, even excluding fast-growing India and China (although, given the population of these two countries, their inclusion is important). This year developing country growth is expected to be 6.8 percent for the fifth consecutive year of strong growth. The outlook for 2007 is one of continued strong developing country growth, in spite of higher oil prices. Sub-Saharan Africa deserves particular mention: it has had a full decade of growth, and annual growth in 17 Sub-Saharan Africa countries exceeded 4 percent over the entire decade. These higher growth rates reflect sustained improvement in the quality of developing country policies and institutions (confirmed by the 2003 ARDE and continuing since then).

Poverty Reduction. On poverty, an important conclusion is that the developing world as a whole is predicted to meet the poverty Millennium Development Goal (MDG). The latest projections indicate that the share of the developing country population living on less than $1 per day will fall from 27.9 percent in 1990 to 10.2 percent in 2015. Even in Sub-Saharan Africa, where conflict and HIV/AIDs have affected poverty-reduction efforts, poverty fell from 46.4 percent in 2001 to 44.0 percent in 2002. It is likely that the substantially positive per capita income growth discussed in the previous paragraph has reduced poverty further.

Challenges of Building on This Progress. Notwithstanding this overall positive record, management recognizes that many countries—particularly in Africa and South Asia—are far from achieving many of the MDGs. However, it is much less of a stretch now for Sub-Saharan African countries, for example, to make the jump from the recent rates of growth to the 7 percent rate estimated as necessary for them to meet the poverty MDG. To help countries achieve these higher rates of growth and poverty reduction, the development community needs a better understanding of what works well under what circumstances and how we can better customize support to clients to create jobs and opportunities (the theme of this year's ARDE). In this context, the President has appointed a Commission on Growth and Development, supported by the Bank and other donors,[1] and comprising leading practitioners from government, business, and the policy-making arena. Over a two-year period, the Commission is expected to shed light on the long-run forces underlying growth experiences and highlight the actions—at the national and international levels—most likely to improve developing countries' growth prospects. In addition, the Poverty Reduction and Economic Management Network (PREM) has been developing and implementing a multipronged work program on growth: flagship analytic work (World Bank 2005c, 2005f); capacity building within the Bank (training, dissemination of good practices, and support to country teams, including "growth diagnostics" pilots); and efforts to bring outsiders' views and analytic work into the Bank (PREM conferences and lecture series).

Increasing the Effectiveness of Bank-Supported Programs

The ARDE makes a series of observations on Bank programs, at the level of the Country Assistance Strategy (CAS) and at the level of individual operations. Management would like to comment on country strategies, sectoral support and cross-sectoral synergies, and governance and transparency.

Successful CASs

The ARDE notes that Bank assistance has been effective when it has taken a realistic view of borrowers' political and institutional capacity and has focused on well-specified objectives. In recent years, these issues have been at the center of Bank support. An overview of borrower capacity is now a key element in the design of CASs and lending operations. The CAS sets out the Bank's diagnosis of the country's development situation (political and institutional) and outlines a selective program of planned Bank Group support that is tailored to the country's needs, supporting the government's own development objectives and strategy, and against the backdrop of the Bank's ongoing portfolio and the activities of other development partners.

The Ambition of CASs. According to the ARDE, IEG finds that when CASs overlook capacity, they tend to be too ambitious. Designing strategies and supporting reform programs is not an exact science. CASs support country-owned programs. Projecting the success of strategies requires balancing elements of institutional and political capacity and commitment. A very circumscribed program can end up missing opportunities for reform, as IEG's own evaluations point out. Even in an uncertain political climate, a country that has strong and broad-based commitment across stakeholders may be able to undertake major reforms successfully.

Attribution. The review rightly points out that successful poverty reduction in a country cannot be attributed to Bank assistance alone. The same is true when poverty-reduction efforts are not successful. In management's view, the ARDE analysis of the Bank's impact on poverty does not fully capture the effectiveness of Bank assistance in helping countries achieve pro-poor growth. This is so because the ARDE analysis uses IEG's ratings of outcomes of Bank-supported country assistance programs drawn from its Country Assistance Evaluations or outcome ratings in undisclosed CAS Completion Report reviews. Outcomes at the country level depend on more than Bank performance. They depend on the performance of other donors, luck—good or bad—and, most important (as the ARDE notes), the quality of the country's own policies, notably economic management. The subjective rating of outcomes is also a difficult task.

Distributional Impacts. The ARDE argues that the Bank has not paid sufficient attention to the distributional effects of growth-enhancing reforms. Management would note that issues around income distribution are not new to the Bank: there is a tradition of work on these issues, and that work has accelerated over the last five years and is perhaps not yet reflected in IEG findings. A notable example is Bank support for Poverty and Social Impact Assessments in countries in all six Bank Regions, with particular focus on Africa. These analyses have covered issues in infrastructure, the public sector, social sectors, macroeconomic reform, and the agricultural sector (World Bank 2006i).[2] Another major change is tied to the updated policy on development policy lending (OP 8.60). Since it was adopted in September 2004, the vast majority of development policy operations have included a review of possible negative poverty and social impacts and, where necessary, mitigation measures (World Bank 2006d). Beyond operations, the Bank has produced major analytic and research work on income distribution and growth, notably the 2006 *World Development Report* (WDR), *Equity and Development* (World Bank 2003b, 2005k, 2006h). On July 11, 2006, management reported to the Bank's executive directors on the activities with which the Bank is operationalizing the messages of the 2006 WDR: support to Regions on operations and analysis, larger-scale pilot programs in support of several countries, and a three-year programmatic research agenda.

The Challenge of Rural Poverty in CASs. The ARDE notes that in most countries examined by IEG evaluations, poverty reduction has been greater in urban than in rural areas, and it links that finding to Bank support being skewed in favor of urban areas. Again, recent information shows progress, notably since the adoption of the Bank's new rural strategy in 2003 (World Bank 2003a). First, countries are taking rural poverty seriously. A review by Bank rural staff shows that of the 17 country-owned Poverty Reduction Strategies prepared in fiscal 2004–05, all included detailed rural poverty diagnoses and 13 mentioned national rural development plans. Within the Bank, 88 percent of CASs prepared in fiscal 2005 had a satisfactory rating for rural poverty diagnosis. Lending is up; lending for rural development was 14 percent of total lending commitments in fiscal 2006. Finally, operational quality is now strong. Recent IEG data show that 84 percent of rural lending operations recently exiting the portfolio were rated satisfactory in terms of development objectives. The latest Quality Assurance Group (QAG) quality-at-entry study shows 87 percent of rural operations as satisfactory at entry—a good predictor of operational success. The 2007 WDR currently under preparation will help hone further our knowledge on how best to support rural and agricultural development. It will provide more clarity on customizing agricultural strategies to specific country conditions and dealing with the risks posed by heavy and often unpredictable government intervention in agricultural export markets.

Strategies in Support of Fragile States. The ARDE notes that in state building, which is now a central focus of the Bank in low-income countries under stress (LICUS), the Bank needs to demonstrate how past weaknesses will be avoided. Regarding state building, management notes that we are learning from the experience of the past, when the international community was too ready to ignore the task of making state institutions more effective and accountable to their people, focusing instead on delivering quick fixes through parallel and unsustainable structures. Management also notes that in-country harmonization among donors in fragile states—although it remains a challenging task— is making significant progress. There are several good examples, such as the use of shared transitional results frameworks in the Central African Republic, Haiti, and Liberia, and joint country strategies completed or under way in gradual reform environments such as Cambodia and Nigeria, as well as in countries with more severe issues, such as the Central African Republic, the Democratic Republic of Congo, Somalia, and Togo. In general, the ARDE does not recognize the significant progress the international community has made in the last three years in its support to fragile states.

Sectoral Support and Cross-Sectoral Synergies and Complementarities

The ARDE notes that the overall performance of the Bank portfolio has increased over the last few years but does not highlight how important that is. While country focus (doing the right things) is key, there is no substitute for quality operations (doing things right). There has been a substantial improvement in the quality at entry of operations: 92 percent of the projects

reviewed received a moderately satisfactory rating or better in the latest quality-at-entry assessment (World Bank 2006j). IEG's project ratings at completion show a continuation of the longer-term improvement in project results (for example, of the fiscal 2005 cohort of operations rated so far, outcomes are rated satisfactory for 82 percent of projects by number and 87 percent weighted by disbursements). The ARDE does not note the substantial improvements in LICUS operations. In 2005, projects in LICUS actually achieved higher levels of performance than projects in non-LICUS low-income countries. While this record may not be sustainable in these difficult environments, the situation is a vast improvement over the 50 percent satisfactory ratings of LICUS operations in fiscal 2002, before the LICUS Initiative began.

Bank Lending Support. Management notes that this strong operational quality performance has been achieved with higher lending from the International Bank for Reconstruction and Development (IBRD) and increased credits and grants from the International Development Association (IDA). In fiscal 2006, IDA provided $9.5 billion in support to poor countries, more than ever before, with more than half going to Sub-Saharan Africa. Because of IDA's performance-based allocation system, those funds are likely to be used effectively by the recipient countries for development and poverty reduction. One of IDA's successes has been to channel funds to better-performing countries and, perhaps even more important, to help align overall donor support behind country-owned growth and poverty-reduction programs. IDA remains central to support for the development process in low-income countries. At the same time, the IBRD's fiscal 2006 lending to middle-income countries—home to two-thirds of the world's poor people—was at its highest level in seven years at $14.2 billion. The new strategy for a stronger Bank Group engagement in IBRD countries is designed to help the Bank engage even more productively with these countries.

Sectoral Synergies. IEG's analysis suggests that in sectoral work the Bank has not paid sufficient attention to the inputs required from other sectors to achieve the outcomes of its interventions. There have been several advances in recent years with regard to cross-sectoral synergies. The IEG review points out examples of operations that successfully achieved these synergies: In Bangladesh, Bank support for female secondary education has contributed to reductions in child mortality; rural electrification operations in general have contributed to improved health outcomes; and rural roads in Morocco have led to increases in agricultural activity and increases in enrollment in primary education. Sector groups have been working to increase the set of operations that achieve these synergies. In fiscal 2005 the Water Supply and Sanitation Sector Board developed a toolkit jointly with PREM to improve the integration of water supply and sanitation policy reforms and implementation arrangements into poverty-reduction support credits. Then, in recognition of the fact that water supply and sanitation services are key to achieving improved health outcomes (for example, in reducing child mortality), in fiscal 2005 the health and infrastructure sectors also launched an important initiative to assess the burden of disease and develop tools for setting priorities. The approach paper *Strategy for Health, Nutrition, and Population,* discussed by CODE in June 2006 (World Bank 2006o), proposed a diagnostic tool—the Binding Constraints on Outcome Improvement (to be piloted) that would highlight the possible gains from enhanced coordination between sectors to achieve health goals. More generally, the Bank's Results Secretariat has worked with networks in the development of over a dozen results-oriented sector strategies. The Secretariat seeks to strengthen the results chains in these strategies in several ways: (a) ensuring that objectives are realistic; (b) identifying important synergies between the Bank's interventions in the sector and in other sectors to achieve the objectives, and designing a strategy to exploit these synergies; and (c) ensuring that the results chain is based on solid evidence about what gets results. The challenge, as IEG correctly points out, is to adapt the results chains to country strategies; and the Results-Based CAS is the tool for meeting that challenge.

Support for Education. IEG notes that in many low-income countries, the objective of ensuring by 2015 that every child completes primary school education has led to massive efforts to build more schools and provide more educational materials, but that rapid expansion in coverage has often been at the expense of attention to learning outcomes. While the importance of expanding enrollment was critical and should not be underestimated, it is true that improvements in learning outcomes have lagged, and countries now need to put as much effort into improving learning outcomes as has gone into getting children into school. The Bank is scaling up its work in this area to help countries improve learning outcomes, as is the overall donor community. Improvement of education quality is now a central part of the endorsement for Fast Track Initiative support, and countries have taken this on board, as noted at the recent Special Ministerial Roundtable on Education at the Annual Meetings in Singapore (World Bank 2006l). Additional activities include programs to increase incentives to focus on learning outcomes and strengthening capacity to measure outcomes and to benchmark them internationally.

Governance and Transparency

IEG concludes that public sector reform initiatives have not always been aligned with political realities and that the progress of Bank-supported reform programs in public administration and public financial management has been slow because of lack of political support. IEG also finds that the Bank has focused excessively on passage of laws and has given insufficient attention to enforcement. Management notes that much has changed in recent years.

Transparency and Related Reforms. In the past decade, the Bank has recognized that reform of the civil service administration can take a long time and that it is not enough merely to ask for passage of laws. Thus, more recent operational support has focused on service-oriented approaches to improving governance and service provision: (a) using public expenditure reviews to highlight sectoral spending priorities; (b) engaging via sectorwide programs; (c) using information to improve accountability for service provision on the ground; (d) decentralizing to shift responsibility for service provision to the entities that provide services; and (e) adopting community-based approaches to local infrastructure investments. Management has also worked with development partners to put together and implement a public financial management performance measurement framework[3] that is more objective than previous perception measures. Early experience with the tool is encouraging.

Doing Business. Regulatory red tape is associated with poor governance and corruption. A thriving, open, and competitive private sector can be a strong source of demand for better governance. The Bank's *Doing Business Report* (World Bank 2006g) benchmarks business regulation in 175 economies. Follow-up work generated by country discussions has led to policy reform, for example, in Bangladesh.

Community-Driven Development. Even when opportunities for governance reform at the national level are limited, the Bank has taken advantage of entry points at the local level through community-driven development, especially when such an approach also supports the development of local government capacity and accountability. The ARDE cites two Bank operations, one in Zambia and the other in Honduras, as good examples. In a related area, management would dispute what the ARDE says about the role of municipal councils in Brazil (page 42). There is substantial evidence that these municipal councils have contributed to (a) engaging local officials in decision making; (b) enhancing local governments' capacities to identify, appraise, and supervise subprojects; and, most important, (c) strengthening local governments' ability to effectively engage local communities and increase government accountability to them.

Engagement in Supporting Good Governance and Anticorruption. There is a general consensus that better governance and stronger anticorruption efforts are central to meeting the MDGs. The Development Committee noted that the principal objective of the Bank's governance work should be to develop capable and accountable states to deliver services to the poor, promote private sector–led growth, and tackle corruption effectively (Development Committee 2006). They supported the Bank's engagement in governance and anticorruption work. The strategy set out in the Bank's paper *Strengthening Bank Group Engagement on Governance and Anticorruption* (World Bank 2006m), building on a decade of global experience and evidence, implies a change in how the Bank Group does business: providing incentives to managers and staff to engage proactively on the ground on governance issues; addressing staffing, skills, and resource needs to operate effectively in challenging governance settings; and developing a stronger results framework. The Bank will now further refine and implement the strategy and report periodically on results.

Conclusions

As noted in the introduction, management finds many of the suggestions by IEG to be constructive. Its recommendations are intuitive: focus on the nature of growth, better articulate results chains to achieve sector outcomes, and provide a realistic assessment of the political economy of governance-related reforms. The Bank is addressing all three as it continues the process of improving Results-Based CASs. With regard to the pattern of growth, the work designed to operationalize the WDR on poverty and inequality is feeding into the CAS process, which often already benefited from Poverty and Social Impact Analysis. IEG suggests a blend of Bank-supported activities across sectors to support CAS objectives, and management agrees, while at the same time noting, as IEG also suggests, being selective in the activities the Bank supports, given budget constraints, and for IDA, a constrained financing capacity. With regard to governance, IEG suggests ensuring that partner countries own the reform approach and pace supported by the Bank, and management agrees. CAS preparation and consultations are key in making these assessments, and this process will be reinforced with the implementation of the governance and anticorruption strategy. The upcoming review of sectoral and country strategies in fiscal 2007 will address progress across these three important dimensions for getting results from Bank assistance.

ENDNOTES

Executive Summary

1. Despite the gravity of events in Timor during 2006, management would note that, outside of the security sectors, Timor's institutions have proven resilient in the face of political crisis and that the new transitional government is committed to involving community institutions in recovery. The international community's response also demonstrates that it has learned that a rapid and coordinated response is a critical factor in supporting countries that meet setbacks in fragile post-conflict transition processes.

2. Management would repeat its finding, noted in the Management Response to the 2005 OED report on *The Effectiveness of World Bank Support for Community-Based and -Driven Development: An OED Evaluation,* cited as IEG 2005i in this report. Management finds that many of its most innovative operations are designed to combine decentralization initiatives with CDD operations to improve local governance. The programs are based on the operational lessons that empowered local communities are able to hold local government accountable for service delivery, improve local government capacity to deliver effective and demand-responsive services. Management notes that the issue of strengthening local government is standard now in the preparation of CDD operations.

3. Management notes that the chairman's summary of the World Bank Executive Directors' Committee on Development Effectiveness meeting on August 31, 2005, on *The Effectiveness of World Bank Support for Community-Based and -Driven Development: An OED Evaluation,* cited as IEG 2005i in this report, recognized the "important contribution of CDD operations to empowering and helping the poor" and supported "scaling-up bank assistance in response to country demand."

Chapter 2

1. Bourguignon (2004b) and Lopez and Serven (2006) show that the poverty elasticity of distributional changes increases with the level of income and decreases with the level of inequality when income is distributed in a log normal function. They test for log normality of income distribution using large cross-country data sets and find that the log normal distribution applies to household income.

2. The most recent global poverty figures date back to 2002, although more recent data are available for a number of individual countries that have undertaken efforts to monitor living standards on a regular basis.

3. The poverty data presented in this chapter cover approximately seven years, from the mid-1990s onward, with the second observation being between 2001 and 2005, depending on country survey data availability. The number of years between surveys varies by country, from five in many of the transition economies to nine in Turkey. Appendix D provides further details.

4. Management notes that it does not agree that the analysis below captures the effectiveness of World Bank assistance in supporting poverty reduction. The analysis relates outcomes as rated by IEG in countries supported by the World Bank to poverty reduction. As the review itself notes, poverty reduction cannot be attributed to Bank support alone. The reverse also holds. Poverty increases cannot be attributed to Bank support alone. Outcomes in countries are the result of support from the Bank; support from other donors (often larger in dollar terms than Bank support); sheer luck (good or bad); but, most important, the country's own performance. That point is effectively made in chapter 2 of the review.

5. Management notes that it believes that the measure of selectivity used by IEG is not well defined

and is overly subjective. It is often the issue most disputed in discussions between management and IEG on IEG country evaluations. Management would also note that IEG's judgment of over-ambition of a CAS may be based on virtually the same factors as its judgment that the outcome was unsatisfactory, calling into question its separate usefulness as a tool for analysis.

6. Based on IEG analysis of World Bank 2005b; IEG 2006r.

7. Based on IEG analysis of World Bank 2005d.

8. While the incidence of poverty remains higher in rural than in urban Brazil, the absolute number of poor living in urban areas is higher than that in rural areas, due to high urbanization.

9. Management notes that the discussion below seems to imply that the Bank has been inactive around issues of equity in development. There has been a long tradition of work on these issues within the Bank, including support over the last five years for Poverty and Social Impact Assessments in literally dozens of countries across the world (see World Bank 2006i). Since the adoption in September 2004 of the updated policy on Development Policy Lending (OP 8.60), the vast majority of these operations have included a review of possible negative poverty and social impacts and, where necessary, mitigation measures (see World Bank 2006d). Most recently, management has produced several analytical and research reports on income distribution and growth, notably the *2006 World Development Report* (WDR), *Equity and Development*. Management reported to Bank executive directors on July 11, 2006, on the set of activities that are in motion to operationalize the messages of the 2006 WDR. These activities include support to Regions on operations and analysis, larger-scale pilot programs in support of several countries, and, importantly, a three-year programmatic research agenda because despite IEG's message in this section, there is still much that the development community needs to learn to understand what works and what does not work in achieving equitable growth.

10. Good macroeconomic management, a higher physical and human capital stock, well-developed financial markets, better-developed infrastructure, stronger institutions, and more trade openness are associated with more robust growth. The relative importance of various pro-growth policies depends, however, on country-specific conditions.

11. See, for example, World Bank 2006h, which estimates that income transfers, including pension systems, lower the Gini coefficient in the core OECD countries by 15 percentage points. Similarly, Atkinson (2004) finds that income transfers lower the Gini coefficient of inequality in the United Kingdom by 18 percentage points.

12. A key feature of Bank operations in support of conditional cash transfer programs is that they have included impact evaluations in program design. Doing so allows for an assessment of targeting effectiveness as well as of the impact on human capital formation. The evaluation results can then be used to improve program design, increase transparency and accountability, and ensure broad-based political support. The World Bank has been instrumental in promoting the use of evaluations in these programs.

13. Management would note that an important improvement acknowledged by the IEG report cited in this paragraph relates to the Bank's portfolio performance in LICUS. The percentage of closed projects rated satisfactory by IEG increased from 50 percent in fiscal 2002, before the LICUS Initiative, to 58 percent in 2003, 65 percent in 2004, and 82 percent in 2005. Regarding state building, management notes that this reflects a need to learn the lessons of the past, when the international community was too ready to ignore the task of making state institutions more effective and accountable to their people, focusing instead on delivering quick fixes through parallel and unsustainable structures. Management also notes that while it remains challenging, in-country harmonization among donors in LICUS is making significant progress. There are several good examples, such as the use of shared transitional results frameworks in the Central African Republic, Haiti, and Liberia, and joint country strategies completed or under way in gradual reform environments such as Cambodia and Nigeria as well as more severe LICUS such as the Central African Republic, the Democratic Republic of Congo, Togo, and Somalia. In general, the comments on page 19 do not recognize the significant progress made by the international community in the last three years in its support to fragile states.

14. Based on IEG analysis of World Bank 2005j.

Chapter 3

1. The analysis excludes the poverty reduction and social development sector boards because IEG has

evaluated very few projects managed by these sector boards. For fiscal 2001–05, IEG evaluated 9 projects managed by the poverty reduction sector board and 13 projects managed by the social development sector board. IEG did not evaluate any projects managed by the two sector boards during fiscal 1996–2000.

2. Management notes that the improvement in portfolio performance was particularly strong in LICUS environments. The percentage of closed projects rated satisfactory by IEG increased from 50 percent in fiscal 2002, before the LICUS Initiative, to 58 percent in 2003, 65 percent in 2004, and 82 percent in 2005. In 2005, projects in LICUS actually achieved higher levels of performance than projects in non-LICUS low-income countries. There is no guarantee that this will be sustained (and indeed it is surprising given the surrounding policy environment), but it is a testament to the efforts of country teams working under difficult conditions.

3. A recent IEG evaluation of the Bank's support for trade found that while earlier on the lack of attention to the poverty and employment effects of trade-related interventions supported by the Bank was due to low prioritization, this no longer seems to be the case. Bank staff now show a considerable interest in the links between trade and poverty, but the difficulty in incorporating poverty considerations into analytical and advisory activities and project design is caused by a combination of not having the right expertise at the operational level; the complexity of the issue, which requires multidisciplinary teams cutting across the Bank's sector network boundaries; and, in some cases, lack of data to underpin the required analysis (IEG 2006c).

4. Many Bank-supported HIV/AIDS projects and national AIDS programs have used stable or declining HIV prevalence (the percent of the population that is HIV-positive) as an indicator of the impact of prevention activities. However, HIV prevalence can rise or fall, depending on whether more people become infected than die over a given period. For example, HIV prevalence can fall if the number of new infections is rising rapidly, but the mortality rate is rising even faster. It can rise, even if the number of new cases is declining, if treatment programs are effectively keeping AIDS patients alive much longer. Thus, to assess success in HIV prevention, countries need to track the number of new infections (HIV incidence) or proxies for it; for success in treatment, they need to track indicators that directly measure health outcomes, such as the mortality rate.

5. Based on an IEG analysis of World Bank 2004b, 2005e.

6. A Sectorwide Approach (SWAp) is an approach to support a locally owned, coherent program for a sector in a comprehensive and coordinated manner, with greater use of country systems. SWAps embody a process that is guided by a set of principles, progressing over time from government leadership toward increased harmonization of implementation mechanisms and use of country systems. SWAps encompass a whole sector or a major sub-sector (such as primary or secondary education). SWAps are characterized by sustained, country-led partnership among development partners and key stakeholders in support of country-owned sector policies and strategies. SWAps promote increasing reliance on country systems and procedures and employ a common framework for planning, implementation, expenditure, and monitoring and evaluation. The Bank has supported SWAps through a variety of lending instruments, depending on the country and sector. Thus the SWAp is an approach to support a government's program in a particular sector, rather than a lending instrument per se.

7. The review involved analysis of IEG ICR Reviews and Project Performance Assessment Reports, IEG case studies covering SWAps in Africa under the IEG Evaluation of Capacity Building in Africa, and World Bank ICRs of SWAps completed over the last three fiscal years in health, education, agriculture, and transport.

Chapter 4

1. It must be noted that most governance indicators currently available, some of which are presented in this report, are perception indicators. While such indicators are useful, they are subject to wide margins of error and must be used with caution. Changes in perception could also come from greater awareness of underlying governance problems, rather than a deterioration or lack of improvement. Furthermore, these perception indicators reflect symptoms of bad governance. They do not directly reveal the quality of government processes, which Bank-supported reforms often aim to improve. The impact of such process changes takes time to manifest itself and affect perception.

2 Based on IEG analysis of World Bank 2006c .

3. Management notes that the observations here are based on a case study of the CDD experience in

Rio Grande do Norte, to which management has expressed numerous substantive disagreements on the methodology and on the interpretation of the data. On the specific issue of municipal councils, the Bank has not contributed to a proliferation of ad hoc councils that bypass local governments, as the review states. Rather, the Bank has helped to establish participatory municipal councils throughout the Northeast that (a) are quite uniform in their structure and operating procedures, (b) engage local governments formally as active participating members, and (c) in most of the states are increasingly serving as an essential decision-making vehicle for the delivery of non-project resources and services. Precisely because of their established effectiveness and transparency, municipal councils are being used increasingly by other state and federal government programs as the vehicle for prioritizing public investments and channeling resources to rural areas. Other councils and coordinating bodies have actually been integrated with the Bank-supported municipal councils, and in that way are serving as an instrument of integration, rather than a cause of fragmentation, as the IEG report states. In sum, management has substantial evidence that municipal councils have actually contributed to (i) the engagement of local officials in decision making; (ii) enhancement of local governments' capacities to identify, appraise, and supervise sub-projects; and, most important, (iii) strengthen the ability of local governments to effectively engage local communities and increase their accountability to them.

Appendix A

1. Data for this appendix include project evaluations conducted through September 15, 2006. Evaluated projects that exited the Bank's portfolio in fiscal 2006 have been excluded from the trend analysis given the low coverage of this fiscal year.

2. The Bank prepares an Implementation Completion Report (ICR) for each lending operation it finances. The ICR is prepared at the time of project completion by the staff of the responsible Regional office (within six months of the final disbursement of the Bank loan). It assesses: (a) the degree to which the project achieved its development objectives and outputs as set out in the project documents; (b) other significant outcomes and impacts; (c) prospects for the project's sustainability; and (d) Bank and borrower performance, including compliance with relevant Bank safeguard and business policies. It also provides the data and analysis to substantiate these assessments, and it identifies the lessons learned from implementation.

The borrower prepares and provides the Bank with its own evaluation report on the project's execution and initial operation, its cost and benefits, the Bank's and borrower's performance, and the extent to which the purposes of the loan were achieved. The borrower's report is attached, unedited, to the ICR.

Once sent to the Board of Executive Directors, each ICR is evaluated by IEG, which validates or adjusts the ratings based on the information provided in the ICR and other operational documents. IEG summarizes its findings in an ICR Review. This review conveys the IEG ratings, comments on the lessons to be drawn and on the quality of the ICR, and suggests whether the project is a candidate for a Project Performance Assessment Report (PPAR). Bank Regional staff have an opportunity to review this summary before it is completed.

The purpose of a PPAR is to validate the findings and augment the information in the ICR and to examine issues and lessons of broad applicability. Some PPARs are intended to serve as building blocks for broad sector studies or Country Assistance Evaluations. They provide independent, field-based, post-completion verification of a project's implementation and results. They incorporate the views of the borrower and main stakeholders, and analyze the operation in its sectoral and country context. The operational staff and borrower representatives have an opportunity to comment on the draft report. The final report is submitted to the Bank's Board and is widely distributed within the Bank and the borrowing country.

3. One project was not classified as either development policy lending or an investment operation.

4. IEG's measure of outcome considers three factors: relevance, efficacy, and efficiency. Relevance measures the expected development impact of a project design by weighing the continuing relevance a project's objectives. Efficacy refers to the extent to which each objective was achieved, or is expected to be achieved. Efficiency measures the cost-effectiveness of a project, based mainly on sectorwide best practices and indicators, where available. Combining these three factors, overall outcome is rated on a six-point scale, ranging from highly satisfactory to highly unsatisfactory.

5. This partial coverage is noted with dashed lines in all the figures in this appendix and with an asterisk (fiscal 2005*). Lending includes IBRD/IDA, Global Environment Facility, Montreal Protocol, and Special Financing.

6. IEG's sustainability measure assesses the resilience to risk of net benefit flows over time by answering the following questions: At the time of evaluation, what is the resilience to risks affecting future net benefit flows? How sensitive is the intervention to changes in the operating environment? Will the intervention continue to produce net benefits as long as intended, or even longer? How well will the intervention weather shocks and changing circumstances?

7. IEG's institutional development impact measure evaluates the extent to which an intervention improves the ability of a country or region to make more efficient, equitable, and sustainable use of its human, financial, and natural resources. Such improvements can derive from changes in values, customs, laws and regulations, and organizational mandates. Accountability, good governance, the rule of law, and the participation of civil society and the private sector are prominent characteristics of an effective institutional environment.

8. The analysis excludes the poverty reduction and social development sector boards because IEG has evaluated very few projects managed by these sector boards. For fiscal 2001–05, IEG evaluated 9 projects managed by the poverty reduction sector board and 12 projects managed by the social development sector board. For fiscal 1996–2000, IEG did not evaluate any projects managed by the poverty reduction and social development sector boards.

9. Some of the PRSC outcome ratings are based on simplified ICRs, and are thus provisional. They are being revisited with full ICRs.

Appendix F

1. These donors include the Swedish, Netherlands, and United Kingdom governments and the William and Flora Hewlett Foundation.

2. See World Bank 2006i, a series of case studies illustrating PSIA in agriculture, energy, utilities, social sectors, taxation, and macroeconomic modeling.

3. See World Bank 2005g. PEFA is a multi-agency partnership program sponsored by the World Bank, the International Monetary Fund, the European Commission, the U.K. Department for International Development, the French Ministry of Foreign Affairs, the Royal Norwegian Ministry of Foreign Affairs, the Swiss State Secretary for Economic Affairs, and the Strategic Partnership with Africa.

BIBLIOGRAPHY

Atkinson, A. 2004. "Increased Income Inequality in OECD Countries and the Redistributive Impact of the Government Budget." In G. Cornia, ed., *Inequality, Growth and Poverty in an Era of Liberalization and Globalization.* Oxford, U.K.: Oxford University Press.

Attanasio, Orazio, Erich Battistin, Emla Fitzsimons, Alice Mesnard, and Marcos Vera-Hernandez. 2005. "How Effective Are Conditional Cash Transfers? Evidence from Colombia." *IFS Briefing Note 54.* London: Institute for Fiscal Studies.

Bellver, Anna, and Daniel Kaufmann. 2005. *Transparenting Transparency: Initial Empirics and Policy Application.* Washington, DC: World Bank.

Bourguignon, Francois. 2004a. "The Growth Elasticity of Poverty Reduction: Explaining Heterogeneity across Countries and Time Periods." World Bank Working Paper 28104. Washington, DC.

———. 2004b. "The Poverty-Growth-Inequality Triangle, Proceedings of the AFD-EUDN Conference 2003." *Notes and Documents* 10.

Cardoso, Eliana, and Souza Andre Porte. 2004. *The Impact of Conditional Cash Transfers on Child Labor and School Attendance in Brazil.* Working Paper No. 04-W07. Nashville, TN: Department of Economics, Vanderbilt University.

Chhibber, Ajay, and Gaurav Nayyar. 2006. "Explaining the Cross-Country Variation in the Growth Elasticity of Poverty." Independent Evaluation Group, World Bank, Washington, DC. Photocopy.

Christiaensen, Luc, Lionel Demery, and Jesper Kühl. 2006. *The Role of Agriculture in Poverty Reduction – An Empirical Perspective.* World Bank Policy Research Paper 4013. Washington, DC.

Collier, Paul, and David Dollar. 2004. "Development Effectiveness: What Have We Learned?" *The Economic Journal* 114, June.

Datt, Gaurav, and Martin Ravallion. 2002. *Is India's Economic Growth Leaving the Poor Behind?* Washington, DC: World Bank.

Deaton, Angus, and Valerie Kozel. 2005. "Data and Dogma: The Great Indian Poverty Debate." *The World Bank Research Observer* 20(2):177–99.

Devarajan, Shantayanan, and Ijaz Nabi. 2006. "Economic Growth in South Asia: Promising, Un-equalizing,...Sustainable?" World Bank, South Asia Region, Washington, DC.

Development Committee. 2006. "Statements Submitted to the Seventy-Fourth Meeting of the Development Committee." DC2006-0021. Singapore.

Dollar, David, and Aart Kraay. 2001. *Growth Is Good for the Poor.* World Bank Policy Research Working Paper 2587. Washington, DC.

Ferreira, Francisco, Phillippe Leite, and Julie Litchfield. 2006. *The Rise and Fall of Brazilian Inequality: 1981–2004.* Washington, DC: World Bank.

Gertler, Paul. 2004. "Do Conditional Cash Transfers Improve Child Health? Evidence from PROGRESA's Control Randomized Experiment." *Health, Healthcare and Economic Development* 94(2).

IEG-World Bank (Independent Evaluation Group-World Bank). Forthcoming. *The Effectiveness of World Bank Fiduciary Assessment.* Washington, DC: World Bank.

———. 2006a. *2006 Annual Report on Operations Evaluation.* IEG Study Series. Washington, DC: World Bank.

———. 2006b. *2005 Annual Report on Operations Evaluation.* IEG Study Series. Washington, DC: World Bank.

———.2006c. *Assessing World Bank Support for Trade, 1987–2004: An IEG Evaluation.* IEG Study Series. Washington, DC: World Bank.

———.2006d. *Debt Relief for the Poorest: An Evaluation Update of the HIPC Initiative.* IEG Special Study. Washington, DC: World Bank.

———. 2006e. *From Schooling Access to Learning Outcomes, An Unfinished Agenda.* IEG Study Series. Washington, DC: World Bank.

———. 2006f. *Honduras Country Assistance Evaluation.* Washington, DC: World Bank.

———. 2006g. *IEG Review of World Bank Assistance for Financial Sector Reform.* IEG Study Series. Washington, DC: World Bank.

———. 2006h. *Madagascar Country Assistance Evaluation.* Washington, DC: World Bank.

———. 2006i. *Malawi Country Assistance Evaluation.* Washington, DC: World Bank.

———. 2006j. *Pakistan County Assistance Evaluation.* IEG Study Series. Washington, DC: World Bank.

———. 2006k. *Pension Reform and the Development of Pension Systems: An Evaluation of World Bank Assistance.* IEG Study Series. Washington, DC: World Bank.

———. 2006l. "Project Performance Assessment Report, Honduras, Third Social Investment Fund Project and Fourth Social Investment Fund Project." Washington, DC, World Bank.

———. 2006m. "Project Performance Assessment Report, Indonesia Second Village Infrastructure Project and Kecamatan Development Project." Washington, DC, World Bank.

———. 2006n. "Project Performance Assessment Report, Nigeria, National Water Rehabilitation Loan, First Multi-State Water Supply Project and Small Towns Water Supply and Sanitation Project." Washington, DC, World Bank.

———. 2006o. "Project Performance Assessment Report, Timor-Leste Community and Local Governance Project and Second Community Empowerment Project." Washington, DC, World Bank.

———. 2006p. "Project Performance Assessment Report, Uganda, District Health Services Pilot and Demonstration Project." Washington, DC, World Bank.

———. 2006q. *Senegal Country Assistance Evaluation.* Washington, DC: World Bank.

———. 2006r. *World Bank Support to Low-Income Countries Under Stress: An IEG Review.* IEG Study Series. Washington, DC: World Bank.

———. 2006s. *Yemen Country Assistance Evaluation.* Washington, DC: World Bank.

———. 2005a. *Albania Country Assistance Evaluation.* Washington, DC: World Bank.

———. 2005b. *2004 Annual Review of Development Effectiveness.* IEG Study Series. Washington, DC: World Bank.

———. 2005c. *Bolivia Country Assistance Evaluation.* Washington, DC: World Bank.

———. 2005d. *Capacity Building in Africa: An OED Evaluation of World Bank Support.* IEG Study Series. Washington, DC: World Bank.

———. 2005e. *Capacity Building in Africa: An OED Evaluation of World Bank Support, Country Case Studies.* IEG Study Series. Washington, DC: World Bank.

———. 2005f. *China: An Evaluation of World Bank Assistance.* IEG Study Series. Washington, DC: World Bank.

———. 2005g. *Committing to Results: Improving the Effectiveness of HIV/AIDS Assistance—An OED Evaluation of the World Bank's Assistance for HIV/AIDS Control.* IEG Study Series. Washington, DC: World Bank.

———. 2005h. *Country Assistance Evaluation Retrospective.* IEG Study Series. Washington, DC: World Bank.

———. 2005i. *The Effectiveness of World Bank Support for Community-Based and -Driven Development.* IEG Study Series. Washington, DC: World Bank.

———. 2005j. *Improving the World Bank's Development Effectiveness: What Does Evaluation Show?* IEG Study Series. Washington, DC: World Bank.

———. 2005k. *Maintaining Momentum to 2015? An Impact Evaluation of Interventions to Improve Maternal and Child Health and Nutrition in Bangladesh.* IEG Study Series. Washington, DC: World Bank.

———. 2005l. *Mauritania Country Assistance Evaluation.* Washington, DC: World Bank.

———. 2005m. *Romania Country Assistance Evaluation*. Washington, DC: World Bank.

———. 2005n. *Turkey Country Assistance Evaluation*. IEG Study Series. Washington, DC: World Bank.

———. 2005o. "Uganda, Sexually Transmitted Infections Project." Project Performance Assessment Report. Washington, DC, World Bank.

———. 2004a. *Armenia Country Assistance Evaluation*. Washington, DC: World Bank.

———. 2004b. *Bhutan Country Assistance Evaluation*. Washington, DC: World Bank.

———. 2004c. *Books, Buildings, and Learning Outcomes: An Impact Evaluation of World Bank Support to Basic Education in Ghana*. IEG Study Series. Washington, DC: World Bank.

———. 2004d. *Brazil Country Assistance Evaluation*. Washington, DC: World Bank.

———. 2004e. *Economies in Transition: An OED Evaluation of World Bank Assistance*. IEG Study Series. Washington, DC: World Bank.

———. 2004f. *Improving the Lives of the Poor Through Investment in Cities: An Update on the Performance of the World Bank's Urban Portfolio*. IEG Study Series. Washington, DC: World Bank.

———. 2004g. *The Poverty Reduction Strategy Initiative*. IEG Study Series. Washington, DC: World Bank.

———. 2004h. "Project Performance Assessment Report. Albania Rehabilitation Credit, Recovery Program Technical Assistance Project, Public Expenditure Support Credit; Structural Adjustment Credit." Washington, DC, World Bank.

———. 2004i. "Project Performance Assessment Report. Cambodia, Disease Control and Health Development Project." Washington, DC, World Bank.

———. 2004j. "Project Performance Assessment Report, Uganda, Primary Education and Teacher Development Project and Education Sector Adjustment Credit." Washington, DC, World Bank.

———. 2003. *Dominican Republic Country Assistance Evaluation*. Washington, DC: World Bank.

———. 2002a. *Peru Country Assistance Evaluation*. Washington, DC: World Bank.

———. 2002b. *Social Funds: Assessing Effectiveness*. IEG Study Series. Washington, DC: World Bank.

———. 2002c. *Zambia Country Assistance Evaluation*. Washington, DC: World Bank.

———. 2001. *India Country Assistance Evaluation*. Washington, DC: World Bank.

IEG-World Bank, -IFC, and -MIGA. 2005. *Extractive Industries and Sustainable Development: An Evaluation of World Bank Group Experience*. IEG Study Series. Washington, DC: World Bank.

———. 2003. *Power for Development: A Review of the World Bank Group's Experience with Private Participation in the Electricity Sector*. IEG Study Series. Washington, DC: World Bank.

Jha, Raghbendra. 2004. "Reducing Poverty and Inequality in India: Has Liberalization Helped?" In *Inequality, Growth and Poverty in an Era of Liberalization*, Giovanni Andrea Cornia, ed. Oxford, U.K., and New York: Oxford University Press. (Also available at http://rspas.anu.edu.au/economics/publish/papers/wp2002/wp-econ-2002-04.pdf)

Kaufmann, Daniel. 2006. "Myths and Realities of Governance and Corruption." In *World Economic Forum, Global Competitiveness Report 2005–2006*. Washington, DC: World Bank.

———. 2003. *Rethinking Governance: Empirical Lessons Challenge Orthodoxy*. Washington, DC: World Bank.

Kaufmann, Daniel, A. Kraay, and M. Mastruzzi. 2005. *Governance Matters IV: Governance Indicators for 1996–2004*. Washington, DC: World Bank.

Korea Educational Development Institute. 2005. *Statistics on Korean Education*. Seoul: KEDI.

Kraay, Aart. 2004. "When Is Growth Pro-Poor? Cross-Country Evidence." World Bank Policy Research Working Paper 3225. Washington, DC.

Levy, H., and C. Voyadzis. 1996. *Morocco Impact Evaluation Report: Socioeconomic Influence of Rural Roads*. Report No. 15808-MOR. Washington, DC: World Bank.

Loayza, Norman, and Claudio Raddatz. 2005. "The Composition of Growth Matters for Poverty Alleviation." World Bank, Washington, DC. Photocopy.

Lopez, Humberto. 2006. "Did Growth Become Less Pro-Poor in the 1990s?" World Bank Policy Research Working Paper 3931. Washington, DC.

———. 2005. "Growth and Inequality. Are They Connected?" Background paper for World Bank, *Pro-Poor Growth in the 1990s: Lessons and Insights from 14 Countries*. Washington, DC, World Bank.

Lopez, J. Humberto, and Luis Serven. 2006. "A Normal Relationship? Poverty, Growth and Inequality." World Bank Policy Research Working Paper 3814. Washington, DC.

Mallucio, J.A., and R. Flores. 2004. "Impact Evaluation of the Pilot Phase of the Nicaraguan Red de Protección Social." Food Consumption and Nutrition Division Discussion Paper 184. Washington, DC: International Food Policy Research Institute.

Mukherjee, Ranjana, and Omer Gokcekus. 2006. "Officials' Asset Declaration Laws: Do They Prevent Corruption?" In *Global Corruption Report*. Berlin and London: Transparency International.

OED (Operations Evaluation Department) Renamed Independent Evaluation Group in December 2005. Please see IEG for publications.

PRS Group. Various years. *International Country Risk Guide*. Syracuse, NY.

Ravallion, Martin. 2004. "Pro-Poor Growth: A Primer." World Bank Policy Research Working Paper 3242. Washington, DC.

———. 2001. "Growth, Inequality and Poverty: Looking Beyond Averages." World Bank Policy Research Working Paper 2558. Washington, DC.

———.1997. "Can High-Inequality Developing Countries Escape Absolute Poverty?" *Economics Letters* 56: 51–57.

Ravallion, Martin, and Shaohua Chen. 2004. *China's (Uneven) Progress Against Poverty*. Washington, DC: World Bank.

———. 2001. "Measuring Pro-Poor Growth." World Bank Policy Research Working Paper 2666. Washington, DC.

Ravallion, Martin, and Gaurav Datt. 1992. "Growth and Redistribution Components of Changes in Poverty Measures: A Decomposition with Applications to Brazil and India in the 1980s." *Journal of Development Economics* 38: 275–95.

Ravallion, Martin, and Emanuela Galasso. 2003. "Social Protection in a Crisis—Argentina's Plan Jefes y Jefas." World Bank Policy Research Working Paper 3165. Washington, DC.

Rawlings, Laura, and Gloria Rubio. 2004. "Evaluating the Impact of Conditional Cash Transfer Programs." *World Bank Research Observer* 20(1): 29–55.

Recanatini, Francesca. Alessandro Prati, and Guido Tabellini. 2005. "Why Are Some Public Agencies Less Corrupt than Others? Lessons from Institutional Reform Survey Data." Paper presented at the Sixth Jacques Polak Annual Research Conference, November 2005, Washington, DC.

Skoufias, Emmanuel. 2005. *PROGRESA and Its Impacts on Welfare of Rural Households in Mexico*. Washington, DC: International Food Policy Research Institute.

Skoufias, Emmanuel, Davis Benjamin, and Sergia De La Vega. 2001. "Targeting the Poor in Mexico: An Evaluation of the Selection of Households into PROGRESA." *World Development* 29(10).

Svensson, Jakob. 2005. "Eight Questions about Corruption." *Journal of Economic Perspectives* 19 (3): 19–42.

Thomas, Vinod, Mansoor Dailami, Ashok Dhareshwar, Daniel Kaufmann, Nalin Kishor, Ramon Lopez, and Yan Wang. 2000. *Quality of Growth*. Washington, DC: World Bank.

World Bank. 2006a. *Accelerating the Results Agenda: Progress and Next Steps*. Washington, DC.

———. 2006b. "BEEPS-at-a-Glance." (Various countries.) Washington, DC.

———. 2006c. "Bulgaria CAS Completion Report. Bulgaria Partnership Strategy Annex C." Washington, DC.

———. 2006d. *Development Policy Lending Retrospective*. Washington, DC.

———. 2006e. *East Asia Update: Solid Growth, New Challenges*. East Asia and Pacific Region, Report No. 35748. Washington, DC.

———. 2006f. *Global Monitoring Report 2006.* Washington, DC.

———. 2006g. *How to Reform.* Doing Business Series. Washington, DC.

———. 2006h. *Poverty Reduction and Growth: Virtuous and Vicious Circles.* World Bank Latin American and Caribbean Studies. Washington, DC.

———. 2006i. *Poverty and Social Impact Analysis of Reforms: Lessons and Examples from Implementation.* Washington, DC.

———. 2006j. *Quality at Entry (QEA7): A QAG Assessment.* Washington, DC.

———. 2006k. *Senegal, Participatory Local Development Project.* Project Appraisal Document. Washington, DC.

———. 2006l. "Special Ministerial Roundtable on Education," Singapore, September 17. http://web.worldbank.org/WBSITE/EXTERNAL/NEWS/0,,contentMDKL21056301~menuPK:34476~pagePK:34370~piPK:34424~theSitePK:4607,00.html

———. 2006m. "Strengthening Bank Group Engagement on Governance and Anticorruption." Washington, DC.

———. 2006n. *World Development Indicators.* Washington, DC.

———. 2006o. "World Bank Strategy for Health, Nutrition, and Population Results." Background Note for briefing to the Committee on Development Effectiveness on the preparation of the new Bank Health, Nutrition, and Population Strategy. Washington, DC.

———. 2005a. "Burkina Faso CAS Completion Report. Burkina Faso Country Assistance Strategy Annex 7." Washington, DC.

———. 2005b. "Cambodia CAS Completion Report. Cambodia Country Assistance Strategy Attachment 1." Washington, DC.

———. 2005c. *Economic Growth in the 1990s: Learning from a Decade of Reform.* Washington, DC.

———. 2005d. "Georgia CAS Completion Report. Georgia Partnership Strategy Annex 2." Washington, DC.

———. 2005e. "Implementation Completion Report: Burkina Faso Poverty Reduction Support Credit IV." Washington, DC.

———. 2005f. *Pro-Poor Growth in the 1990s: Lessons and Insights from 14 Countries.* Agence Française de Développement, Bundesministerium für Wirtschaftliche Zusammenarbeit und Entwicklung, U.K. Department for International Development, and the World Bank. Washington, DC.

———. 2005g. "Public Financial Management—Performance Measurement Framework." PEFA Secretariat. Washington, DC.

———. 2005h. *Reducing Poverty on a Global Scale, Learning and Innovating for Development, Findings from the Shanghai Global Learning Initiative,* B. Moreno-Dodson, ed. Case Studies. Washington, DC.

———. 2005i. "Results Focus in Country Assistance Strategies: A Stocktaking of Results-Based CASs." OPCS. Washington, DC.

———. 2005j. "Uruguay CAS Completion Report. Uruguay Country Assistance Strategy Annex 1." Washington, DC.

———. 2005k. *World Development Report 2006: Equity and Development.* Washington, DC; New York: Oxford University Press.

———. 2004a. *World Development Report 2004: Making Services Work for Poor People.* Washington, DC; New York: Oxford University Press.

———. 2004b. "Implementation Completion Report: Burkina Faso Poverty Reduction Support Credit III." Washington, DC.

———. 2003a. *Agriculture and Rural Development: Reaching the Rural Poor.* Washington, DC.

———. 2003b. *Inequality in Latin America and the Caribbean—Breaking with History.* Washington, DC.

———. 2001. *World Development Report 2000/2001: Attacking Poverty.* Washington, DC; New York: Oxford University Press.

ECO-AUDIT
Environmental Benefits Statement

The World Bank is committed to preserving endangered forests and natural resources. The Office of the Publisher has chosen to print ***Annual Review of Development Effectiveness 2006: Getting Results*** on recycled paper with 30 percent post-consumer waste, in accordance with the recommended standards for paper usage set by the Green Press Initiative, a nonprofit program supporting publishers in using fiber that is not sourced from endangered forests. For more information, visit www.greenpressinitiative.org.

Saved:
- 7 trees
- 5 million BTUs of total energy
- 642 lbs. of net greenhouse gases
- 2,664 gallons of waste water
- 342 lbs. of solid waste